A Taste of Mexico
With
Jozi Maldonado

Published by: **The Castaway Company**
                  P.O. Box 531269
                  Harlingen, Texas 78553

ISBN 0-9642308-0-1

A Taste Of Mexico with Jozi Maldonado
is dedicated
to the best cook in the world,
my Mom, Atanacia Maldonado

Table of Contents

Introduction

Welcome to the world of Mexican cooking, the Maldonado way.

There have been several excellent books written over the years about preparing <u>authentic</u> or <u>genuine</u> Mexican cuisine. Although I have been fortunate to have traveled extensively in the country of my family's origin, and some of what is included here came to me that way, most of the content of **A Taste of Mexico** was compiled from what researchers might call "oral history" or "original research."

Simply put, my mother taught me to cook (and my sisters) just as her mother had taught her. My favorite recipes are those that are prepared on a regular basis within our extended family and have been passed down mother to daughter for generations.

Having grown up in Texas, a few miles from the border with Mexico, I can't say that some "Tex-Mex" influence have not been introduced into our kitchens, but the basics of our food preparation have been fairly constant for at least my lifetime.

Preparing Mexican meals is easy and relatively inexpensive. If you are a viewer of my companion television series, you have already seen how much fun it can be.

Although this work is a cookbook, I thought you might enjoy reading about some of my experiences from traveling within Mexico. Invariably, whenever I have returned from a trip, someone will ask, "Weren't you afraid?"

No, I was never afraid. I have felt much safer in Mexico, even in its cities, than I have in many of the places I have visited in the United States.

Another question often asked is if I have ever gotten sick from eating in Mexico. I have felt like riding low in the saddle a few times while away from home, but I am not sure I can blame it directly on anything I ate. Quite truthfully, other than always drinking bottled water and beverages, we took few precautions while traveling and frequently ate tacos bought from street vendors.

Many of the basic ingredients for Mexican cooking were in use by the Aztec civilization when the Spanish arrived in the 1500s. Corn tortillas, beans, tomatoes, and several species of capsicum peppers had been food staples of the indigenous people for centuries. The challenge then was the same one that any cook faces today. How can these ingredients be combined and presented to provide variety, nutrition, and pleasure to the family diet.

The arrival of the Europeans in Mexico had an effect on Mexican cuisine, but the barrage of American influences today is probably changing Mexico even more rapidly. If you have not traveled in Mexico recently, or you have never been there, you might be shocked to see the golden arches of McDonald's, Pizza Hut, and Kentucky Fried Chicken (to name only a few chains) in every city of any size.

Even more compelling is the effect that satellite television and the programming it provides is having on the traditional way of life. A traveler should not be surprised to find young men in most cities wearing Nike tennis shoes and a Dallas Cowboy T-shirt. One can stand in the suburb of virtually any city and count dozens of satellite dishes.

Writing this book has been a pleasure.

I like to think that assembling this cookbook, along with the re-telling of anecdotes about Mexico, have provided a cultural bridge for me and that I now have a better understanding of who I am and what I can contribute.

You'll be entering the Maldonado kitchen whenever you prepare any of these meals. Come on in and enjoy yourself.

Jozi Maldonado

Beans & Vegetables

Black Beans
Frijoles Negros

2 pounds pinto beans
1/2 cup shortening or 1/2 pound bacon
1 garlic clove, crushed
1 onion, chopped
Salt

First clean the beans by taking out all the rocks and broken pieces out. Soak beans in hot water for an hour. Rinse and place beans in a large pot with water and boil. Add the rest of the ingredients. Have a small pot with warm water nearby. Always keep beans covered with water. When water is needed, it is important to add only warm or hot water. Cook for three hours or until tender. Season to taste.

Serves 10

Fried Green Tomatoes
Tomates Fritos

4 green tomatoes
1 cup corn meal
Salt
Pepper
1 cup butter

Cut the tomatoes in thick slices. Put corn meal on a plate and season with salt and pepper. Pat each tomato in the seasoned corn meal. Heat skillet and add butter until it is very hot, but not brown. Pat the tomatoes again in the corn meal and place in the skillet. Fry both sides until golden. Repeat with the rest of the slices. Drain on paper towel. Serve hot.

Serves 4

NOTE: When a recipe calls for Mexican green tomatoes, most of the time that means *tomatillos* are required, which are not a tomato at all. However, the green tomatoes called for in the above recipe are really unripened, green tomatoes.

Fried Potatoes
Papas Fritas

3 potatoes
1/4 cup of onion, chopped
4 strips of bacon
Cooking oil
Salt
Pepper

Wash, peel and dice potatoes. Heat one skillet and fry bacon to taste. Remove bacon and saute onions. Heat another skillet and add oil. On medium heat, add potatoes and cover for ten minutes. Uncover and add the onions and bacon. Stir occasionally and cook until the potatoes are golden brown. Serve with flour tortillas and fried eggs.

Serves 4

Fried Squash

4 medium summer squash, sliced
3 eggs
1/2 cup milk
1/2 teaspoon salt
Pepper
2 cups corn meal
Cooking oil

In a large bowl beat eggs. Then add milk and stir. Mix cornmeal, salt and pepper on a plate. Heat a skillet and add oil. Dip each squash in the egg mixture and pat both sides well in corn meal mixture. Fry until both sides are golden brown and crispy. Soak excess on paper towel.

Serves 6

NOTE: The squash is a member of the gourd family and had its origins in South America. However, use of the plant for food had spread throughout the Americas by the time the Europeans arrived. The squash has remained a popular vegetable in Mexico.

Green Beans And Red Peppers
Ejote con Rajas

1 can green beans, drained
1 tablespoon butter
1 garlic clove, crushed
1 cup red bell pepper, julienned

Heat a skillet and add butter, garlic and julienned slices. Saute until peppers are tender. Add green beans and stir until heated thoroughly. Serve warm with steak of choice.

Serves 4

NOTE: Bell peppers, whether red or green, are sweet rather than hot and apparently take their name from their shape. The full extent of their use in pre-Hispanic times is not known, but their first recorded use was observed in Panama by an English pirate in 1681.

The Mexican Flag
Rajas de Chile Dulce y Cebolla

1 garlic clove
1/8 teaspoon black peppercorns
3 tablespoons olive oil
2 sweet onions, sliced thin
1 green bell pepper, julienned
1 red bell pepper, julienned
Salt

Crush or grind garlic and peppercorns to a smooth paste. Heat a skillet and add oil. Stir in spices. Without mixing, add green peppers on one side, red peppers on another and the onions on another side. Cover and let simmer on low heat for 10 minutes. Stir vegetables without mixing them up. Prepare your favorite Mexican style steak and top with "The Mexican Flag".

Mexican Rice
Arroz Mexicano

1 cup long grain rice
3 tablespoons cooking oil
2 garlic cloves
1/4 teaspoon cumin seeds
1/4 teaspoon black peppercorns
1/4 cup tomato sauce
1/2 tomato, diced
1/4 cup onions, diced
1/4 cup bell pepper, julienned
1 potato, cubed
1 carrot, diced
salt

Crush or grind garlic, cumin and peppercorns. Heat skillet and add oil. Add rice and brown. To this add tomato sauce, spices, tomatoes, onions, and bell peppers. Simmer for a minute. Add two cups of tap water, potatoes and carrots and cover. Cook until rice and veggies are tender. Season to taste. Serve with warm tortillas, beans and a meat of choice.

Serves 4-6

Mexican "Zesty" Roasted Corn
Elotes con Chile

8-10 ears of corn
1/2 cup mayonnaise
1/2 cup sour cream
2 lemons
Cayenne Pepper
Lemon Pepper
Parmesan Cheese

Boiling corn may be substituted instead of roasting. If roasting corn on a barbecue grill, remove corn silks. Leave some of the corn shucks on to keep the corn from burning and drying out. Roast over hot coals for an hour, turning frequently. If parts of the corns actually burn, it is ok, they are still edible. In a small bowl mix mayonnaise and sour cream together. In a separate bowl, squeeze lemons and add enough cayenne pepper until it makes a paste. When the corn is done, remove shucks completely and spread mayonnaise and sour cream mixture. With a brush, lightly spread the lemon and cayenne mixture, this will be very hot so be careful of how much of this goes on the corn. Then sprinkle lemon pepper and Parmesan cheese to your desire. ENJOY!!

Serves 8-10

Onion Rings
Cebollas Fritas

3 onions, cut into rings
1 cup flour or corn meal
2 teaspoons chili powder
Salt
Water
Cooking oil

In a large bowl, mix flour and chili powder. Salt to taste. To this mixture add enough water to make a light batter. Heat skillet and add 1/4 inch thick of oil. Dip onions in batter and fry quickly until crisp. Drain on paper towel. Serve hot with guacamole burgers.

Serves 6-8

Party Pinto Beans
Frijoles a la Charra

2 pounds pinto beans
1/2 cup shortening
2 garlic cloves, crushed
3 tablespoons cooking oil
1 onion, diced
1 tomato, diced
1 cup coriander sprigs
Salt

First clean the beans by taking out all the rocks and broken pieces out. Soak beans in hot water for an hour. Rinse and place beans in a large pot with water and boil. Have a small pot on a low simmer with water. Always keep beans covered with water. When water is needed, it is important to add only warm or hot water. Cook for three hours or until tender. Season to taste. Heat a skillet and add oil. Saute onions, tomatoes, garlic and coriander. Add this mixture to the pot of beans and stir.

Serves 10

Pinto Beans
Frijoles Pintos

2 pounds pinto beans
1/2 cup shortening
1 garlic clove, crushed
1/4 small onion
Salt

First clean the beans by taking out all the rocks and broken pieces out. Soak beans in hot water for an hour. Rinse and place beans in a large pot with water and boil. Add the rest of the ingredients. Have a small pot with warm water nearby. Always keep beans covered with water. When water is needed, it is important to add only warm or hot water. Cook for three hours or until tender. Season to taste.

Serves 10

Potatoes And Mexican Sausage
Papas con Chorizo

3 potatoes
Cooking oil
1 link of Mexican sausage

Wash, peel and dice potatoes. Heat skillet and add oil. Add potatoes and cook on medium heat, covered for ten minutes. In the same skillet, move potatoes to a side and add sausage. Uncover until the sausage is cooked thoroughly, then mix well. Stir occasionally until potatoes are soft. Serve with tortillas.

Serves 4

NOTE: While many cultures learned to preserve meat by drying or salting it, the Mexicans took the pork and smoked sausage know-how brought by the Spanish and developed *chorizo* to suit many regional tastes. The best known *chorizo* is made in the city of Toluca, which is located west of Mexico City.

Refried Beans
Frijoles Refritos

1 1/2 cups cooked pinto or black beans
Ground black pepper
Cooking oil

Heat skillet and add oil. On medium heat, add beans and stir occasionally for five minutes. Mash beans to a smooth consistency. Sprinkle with black pepper. If the mixture is runny add one teaspoon of flour at a time until the mixture is dry and smooth. Serve with warm flour or corn tortillas.

Serves 4

NOTE: Beans are native to Mexico and were a part of the diet of the indigenous people long before the Spanish came. Although most of us who live in the U.S. think of beans as being most often refried, such as the recipe above, there are many unique regional uses of the pinto and black bean in Mexico.

Rice
Arroz

1 cup of long grain rice
3 tablespoons of oil
1/2 tomato, diced
1/4 cup of onions, diced
1/4 cup of bell pepper, julienned
2 garlic cloves
1/4 teaspoon cumin seeds
1/4 teaspoon black peppercorns
1/4 cup tomato sauce
Salt

Crush or grind garlic, cumin and peppercorns. Heat skillet and add oil. Add rice and brown. To this add tomato sauce and simmer for a minute. Add spices and all other ingredients and stir. Add two cups of tap water and cover for twenty minutes on low heat. Season to taste. Serve with warm tortillas, beans and a meat of choice.

Serves 4-6

Squash In Butter Sauce

2 pounds summer squash, sliced
1 garlic clove
1/8 teaspoon black peppercorns
1/4 cup butter
Salt to taste
Oregano to taste

Crush or grind garlic and peppercorns. Heat a skillet and add butter and spices. Then add squash and saute until tender. Sprinkle with salt and oregano to taste. Serve hot with any meat entree.

Serves 4

Stewed Cabbage
Repollo Guisado

1 small cabbage, rinsed
2 garlic cloves
1/2 teaspoon cumin seeds
1/4 teaspoon black peppercorns
3 tablespoons cooking oil
1/4 cup onions, diced
1/4 cup tomato sauce
2 cups water
Salt

Chop cabbage into small pieces. Crush or grind garlic, cumin and peppercorns. Heat skillet and add oil. Saute onions and crushed spices. Add cabbage, tomato sauce and water. Stir well. Cover and simmer until cabbage is tender. Season to taste. Serve hot with flour tortillas.

Serves 4

NOTE: In this work, the English word cumin is used to identify a spice that is often found in recipes from Mexico. However, the Spanish word for it is *Comino* and the spice is often packaged under that label, especially in states on the southern border.

Stewed Cabbage With Beef Tips
Repollo Guisado con Carne

1 small cabbage, rinsed
2 garlic cloves
1/2 teaspoon cumin seeds
1/4 teaspoon black peppercorns
1/2 pound stew meat
3 tablespoons cooking oil
1/4 cup tomato sauce
1/4 cup onions, diced
2 cups water
Salt

Chop cabbage into small pieces. Crush or grind garlic, cumin and peppercorns. Heat skillet and add oil. Then brown meat and add cabbage. Add tomato sauce, onions and crushed spices. Stir and add water. Cover and simmer until cabbage is tender. Season to taste. Serve hot with flour tortillas.

Serves 4

White Rice
Arroz Blanco

1 cup of long grain rice
3 cups hot water
3 tablespoons of oil
1/4 cup onions, diced
2 cloves garlic
1/4 teaspoon cumin seeds
1/4 teaspoon black peppercorns
3 cups chicken broth
Salt

In a large bowl add rice and hot water and let it stand for 20 minutes. Drain and rinse rice with cold water. Crush or grind garlic, cumin and peppercorns. Heat skillet and add oil. Add rice simmer for a minute. Add spices and onions. Stir constantly without letting the rice stick. Add broth and cook uncovered. Cook over medium flame without stirring or it will turn to mush. When the liquid has been absorbed, remove from heat and cover tightly. Let it sit for 20 minutes while the grains expand. Season to taste. Serve with your favorite fish or soup.

Serves 4

Arnold In Paradise

Puerto Vallarta has been the site of several movies. The one that put it on the map for U.S. audiences was"The Night of the Iguana," which starred the late Richard Burton. More recently, it was "The Predator" with Arnold Swartznagger.

When our guide picked us up at the Fiesta Americana Hotel, he insisted that we must visit the site where the latter movie was filmed. When he found that we did not have a rental car at our disposal, he offered to transport us in his 30-year-old Chevy Nova. He neglected to inform us that it had no shocks or that the trunk had been jerked out so that dust off the dirt road would boil up like smoke inside the cab.

Into the rain forest we rode, more primitive and isolated from civilization with each passing mile. We eventually arrived at an outdoor restaurant beside a wading pool where a likeness of Arnold had been etched on plywood. While waiting for our order to be processed, the resident monkey on a rope jumped on my shoulders and tried to take lumps of hair handfuls at a time from my head.

At least the beer was cold.

When we finally got back to civilization, I showered to take the red dirt from every pore of my skin and readied myself for a nice dinner high on the mountain that overlooks Puerto Vallarta. As our taxi passed the Hard Rock Cafe and veered even higher on the steep street, we spied Senor Pepe's.

We were met at the door by the owner's daughter, who also doubled at the piano bar. She asked us to sign the register. On the same page as my signature was that of Arnold, who wrote beside his name, "I'll be back."

And we hope to be, too.

Beef Dishes

Avocado Burgers

2 pounds ground beef
2 cups fresh parsley, chopped
2 cups onion, chopped
2 large eggs
1 tablespoon salt
1/2 cup Parmesan cheese, grated
1/2 teaspoon Tabasco sauce
1 teaspoon black peppercorns, crushed
3 cups bread crumbs
Guacamole (See recipe)

Burger dressings:
Hamburger buns
Lettuce
Tomato
Onions
Pickles
Mustard
Mayonnaise

Mix all ingredients together except bread crumbs and guacamole. Form into balls. Sprinkle bread crumbs on a pastry board and pat each ball into a patty on the bread crumbs. Chill until ready to cook. Grill, bake or fry as desired. Serve each burger with a spoonful of guacamole. Dress each avocado burger as desired.

Serves 4-6

The Maya

There are literally thousands of archeological sites in the State of Yucatan. Many were large cities that included broad streets, water and sewer systems, and even ball courts for entertainment.

Our visit to *Dzibilchaltun*, near Merida, was interesting not as much for the ruins themselves as for what we saw and heard.

Outside of Merida, the inhabitants of this state are virtually all of Maya ancestry. Our guide, for instance, had a Mexican father and a Maya mother. He considered himself of mixed race.

How strange it was as we made our way several hundred yards from the entrance to the Pyramid of the Dolls to see Maya workmen restoring the roads, dwellings, and pyramids that they and the Spanish destroyed hundreds of years ago.

Indeed, after the Spanish were repelled in 1591, it was the Maya who hid the Pyramid of the Dolls, which was built to capture the power of ancient equinoxes, under the rubble from surrounding structures. It was to have been restored when the Spanish were completely defeated.

At a natural *cenote*, or spring, on the grounds of *Dzibilchaltun*, Maya men washed shards of pottery that had been made by their ancestors. I couldn't understand a word of what they said to each other because Maya, not Spanish, is their language of choice.

Our guide told us that most of the younger men learned Spanish so that they could find work in the cities, and sometimes pretended to be Mexican, but when they came home to their families they spoke Maya.

Beef Intestines
Tripas

5 pounds beef intestines
Cooking oil
Salt

Hook each beef intestine to water hose or faucet to clean. Cut into 4 inch pieces. Boil in a large pot, skimming fat frequently. Remove from heat and drain. Heat skillet and add oil and fry several pieces of intestine at a time. Fry until crispy and golden brow set aside on paper towels to blot excess oil. Season to taste. Serve with corn tortillas and a hot sauce of choice.

Serves 4

Beef Quesadillas
Quesadillas de Res

1 pound beef fajitas (See recipe of choice)
6 ounces white cheese of choice
6 flour tortillas
1 cup lettuce, shredded
1 cup tomatoes, diced
1 cup guacamole, (See recipe)
1 cup picante sauce

On medium to high heat, heat *comal* or griddle. Cut cheese in thin strips. Place one tortilla on the griddle and quickly place cheese strips to cover, add beef strips and place a tortilla on top. Toast each side until golden brown or until cheese oozes out. Once cooked, put each quesadilla on a plate and cut in quarters and serve with condiments.

Serves 3

Beef Skirts 1
Fajitas de Res

3-4 pounds of beef skirts*
1 can beer of choice
2 lemons
1/3 cup worcestershire sauce
Salt
Pepper

Take fat off the beef skirts. In a large bowl squeeze lemons, add beer and worcestershire sauce. Let them marinate for one hour, but turn frequently. Season to taste. Grill or bake to your specifications. Cut beef skirts in strips against the grain.

* Chicken breast may be substituted to make chicken fajitas

Serves 8-10

NOTE: Beef skirts must be marinated since it is a tough cut of meat. Meat should be marinated at least one hour or more to blend flavors and soften the meat. Cutting against the grain makes the meat easier to eat after cooking.

Beef Skirts 2
Fajitas de Res

2 pounds of beef skirts*
1/2 can of beer of choice
1 lemon
1/2 onion, chopped
1/2 bell pepper, chopped
1/4 cup of worcestershire sauce
1 teaspoon of liquid smoke
Salt
Pepper

Take fat off the beef skirts. In a large bowl squeeze lemons, and add all ingredients. Let them marinate for one hour, but turn frequently. Season to taste. Grill or bake to your specifications. Cut beef skirts in strips against the grain.

* Chicken breast may be substituted to make chicken fajitas

Serves 4-6

Beef Skirts 3
Fajitas de Res

2 pounds of beef skirts*
1/2 can of beer of choice
1 lemon
1/2 onion, chopped
1 teaspoon liquid smoke
1 1/2 teaspoons cumin seeds
2 large garlic cloves
1/2 teaspoon of black peppercorns
Salt
Pepper

Take fat off the beef skirts. Crush or grind all spices. In a large bowl squeeze lemons, and add all ingredients. Let them marinate for one hour, but turn frequently. Season to taste. Grill or bake to your specifications. Cut beef skirts in strips against the grain.

* Chicken breast may be substituted to make chicken fajitas.

Serves 4-6

Beef Skirts 4
Fajitas de Res

2 pounds of beef skirts*
3/4 cup cooking wine
1/2 onion, chopped
1/2 cup barbecue sauce of choice
Salt
Pepper

Take fat off the beef skirts. In a large bowl add all ingredients. Let them marinate for one hour, but turn frequently. Season to taste. Grill or bake to your specifications. Cut beef skirts in strips against the grain.

* Chicken breast may be substituted to make chicken fajitas

Serves 4-6

Beef Skirts In A Cheese Blanket Serape

2 pounds of beef skirts* (See recipe of choice)
1 garlic clove
1/2 teaspoon cumin seeds
1/8 teaspoon black peppercorns
1 tomato, diced
1 onion, julienned
1/2 green bell pepper, julienned
1 cup Monterrey Jack cheese, shredded
Cooking oil
1/4 cup water
Salt
Pepper

Take fat off the beef skirts. Crush or grind all spices. Heat skillet and add oil. Add beef skirts, spices, tomato, onions and bell peppers. Add water and cook meat as desired. Season to taste. Add cheese and cover until it melts. Serve with hot tortillas and a bowl of beans. Serve with hot tortillas and a bowl of beans.

Serves 4-6

Beef Skirt Tortilla Crepe Chimichangas de Fajita

1-2 pounds of beef skirts (See recipe of choice)
1 garlic clove
1/2 teaspoon cumin seeds
1/8 teaspoon of black peppercorns
1 tomato, diced
1 onion, julienned
1/2 green bell pepper,
1 cup Monterrey Jack cheese, shredded
Cooking oil
1/4 cup water
Salt
Pepper
Flour tortilla dough of choice
Lettuce, shredded
Tomato, diced
Sour Cream
Guacamole

Take fat off the beef skirts. Crush or grind all spices. Heat skillet and add oil. Add beef skirts, spices, tomato, onions and bell peppers. Add water and cook meat as desired. Season to taste. Take out beef skirts and chop finely. Fold out tortillas and fill each with beef skirts, and cheese then fold over and secure by pinching the sides together. Heat another skillet with 1/4 inch of oil and fry chimichangas until golden brown on both sides. Top with lettuce, tomato, sour cream and guacamole.

Serves 4-6

Beef Skirts With Mushrooms
Fajitas con Champinones

3 pounds beef skirts (See recipe of choice)
2 garlic cloves
1/4 teaspoon of cumin seeds
1/8 teaspoon black peppercorns
1/2 cup bell pepper, julienned
1/2 onion, whole
1/2 cup tomato, diced
2 cups medium picante sauce
2 cups canned mushrooms, not drained
Salt

Crush or grind garlic, cumin and peppercorns. Remove fat from beef and slice in strips, against the grain. In a large sauce pan add beef, spices, julienne slices and onions. Cover and simmer on low heat. If it is too dry, add 1/4 cup water and stir. Add tomatoes and cook on low heat and covered, until meat is tender. Add picante sauce and undrained mushrooms to the beef skirts. Heat thoroughly and season to taste. Serve hot with flour tortillas, rice and beans.

Serves 6

Beef Tongue
Lengua

1 whole cow tongue
All season mix
1/2 onion, diced
1/2 bell pepper, diced
Salt
Pepper
Corn tortillas
Red hot sauce (See recipe)
2 lemons

Prepare tongue by smothering with seasoning. Place tongue in a crockpot with onions, bell peppers and fill half way with water. Add salt and pepper and more seasoning to water. Cook for six hours on low heat. Once it is cooked, take the tongue out of the water and peel the outer layer of the tongue. Shred tongue and serve with corn tortillas and hot sauce. Squeeze lemon juice in each taco.

Serves 8-10

Beef Tortilla Crepes
Chimichangas de Res

Flour tortilla dough (See recipe of choice)
1 pound of stew meat, cubed
1 garlic clove
1/4 teaspoon cumin seeds
1/4 teaspoon black peppercorns
1/4 cup water
Salt
Pepper
Cooking oil
Lettuce, shredded
Tomato, diced
Cheddar cheese, grated
1 pint sour cream
1 cup guacamole, see recipe

Crush garlic, cumin , and peppercorns to a smooth paste. Heat a skillet and add oil. Add meat and brown. Add spices, water and stir well. Cook for 25 minutes on medium heat. Simmer until juices are cooked off. Season to taste. Let the meat cool and dry. Fold out tortillas and fill each with meat then fold over and secure by pinching the sides together. Heat another skillet with 1/4 inch of oil and fry chimichangas until golden brown on both sides. Top with lettuce, tomato, cheese, sour cream and guacamole.

Serves 8-10

Beer Steaks
Bisteces con Cerveza

6 breakfast steaks
Salt
Pepper
Cooking oil
1 cup beer of choice
1 tablespoon tomato paste
1 tablespoon flour
1/2 onion, cut in rings

Season steaks on both sides with salt and pepper. In a bowl add beer, tomato paste and flour. Mix until flour and paste are dissolved. Heat skillet and add oil. Sear steaks with onions then add mixture. Heat thoroughly. Cover and simmer until steaks are done. Serve with refried beans.

Serves 6

Cow Cheek
Barbacoa de Cachete

5 pounds cow cheek
All season mix
1/2 onion, diced
1/2 bell pepper, diced
Salt
Pepper
Corn tortillas
Red hot sauce (See recipe)
2 lemons cut in wedges

Prepare cheek by smothering with seasoning. Place tongue in a crockpot with onions, bell peppers and fill half way with water. Add salt and pepper and more seasoning to water. Cook for six hours on low heat. Once it is cooked, take the meat out of the water. Remove fat and shred meat. Serve with corn tortillas and hot sauce. Squeeze lemon juice in each taco.

Serves 8-10

Cow's Tongue In Tomato Sauce
Lengua

1 whole cow's tongue cooked (See recipe)
1 small onion, diced
1 cup tomato, diced
1/4 cup of bell pepper julienned
1 cup tomato sauce
2 garlic cloves
1/4 cumin seeds
1/4 black peppercorns
1/4 cup water
1/4 cup cooking oil

Crush or grind garlic, cumin and peppercorns. Heat skillet and add oil. Lightly brown tongue. Add spices, tomatoes, tomato sauce, onions, bell peppers and water. Simmer for ten minutes or until done. Season to taste. Serve with warm tortillas and beans.

Serves 4

Liver
Higado

6 liver steaks
1 cup onion, diced
Cooking oil
1 bay leaf
1 cup white wine
Salt
Pepper

Heat skillet and add oil. Saute onion. Add liver and brown lightly. Then add bay leaf and wine. Simmer for 15 minutes. Season to taste. Serve hot with tortillas.

Serves 6

Meat And Potatoes
Papas con Carne

1 pound of stew meat, cubed
2 large potatoes, peeled and diced
1/4 cup tomato, diced
1/4 cup onion, diced
2 garlic cloves
1/4 teaspoon cumin seeds
1/8 teaspoon peppercorns
1 cup water
Oil
Salt

Crush or grind garlic, cumin and pepper corns. Heat skillet and add oil. Brown meat and add potatoes. Add tomatoes, onions, spices and one cup of water and cook until potatoes are tender. Season to taste. Serve with warm flour tortillas and beans.

Serves 4

Meat In Gravy
Carne Guisada

1 1/2 pounds of stew meat, cubed
1 tomato, diced
1 onion, diced
1/2 bell pepper, julienned
3 tablespoons flour
2 garlic cloves
1/4 teaspoon cumin seed
1/4 teaspoon black peppercorns
Salt
Pepper
3 tablespoons cooking oil

Crush or grind garlic cloves, cumin, and pepper corns to a smooth paste. Heat a skillet and add oil. Add meat and brown. Cook for 25 minutes on medium heat. Add tomatoes, onions and bell peppers. Add flour and spices and stir well. To this add one cup of water and let it simmer another five minutes or until meat is tender. Season to taste. Serve with flour tortillas, beans and rice.

Serves 4

Mexican Stew
Caldito

1 pound stew meat
3 potatoes, diced
4 carrots, sliced
3 corn cobs, sliced
1 1/2 cup mixed vegetables, drained
1/2 cup onion, diced
1/2 bell pepper, julienned
Celery, diced
4 ounces tomato sauce
1 teaspoon hot sauce
1 envelope stew seasoning
Flour
Water

In a large pan or pot, brown meat with onion and bell pepper. Add enough flour to cover meat. Add stew seasoning according to instructions on packet. Add all other ingredients, except mixed vegetables. Add water to cover. Cook until vegetables and meat are tender. Add mixed vegetables. Serve with corn bread.

Serves 4

Picadillo 1

1 pound lean ground beef
 1 small potato, peeled and cubed
1 carrot, peeled and cubed
1/4 onion, cubed
1 1/2 tomatoes
1/2 teaspoon vinegar
1 garlic clove
1/4 teaspoon cumin seeds
1/8 teaspoon peppercorns
1 tablespoon oil
Salt
Pepper

Boil potatoes and carrots until tender and drain. Heat skillet and add oil. Saute onions and brown ground beef. Crush or grind garlic, cumin, and peppercorns. In a blender add spices, tomato and vinegar and puree. Pour mixture over meat. Add vegetables and stir. Season to taste. Serve with warm tortillas.

Serves 3

Picadillo 2

1 1/2 pounds lean ground beef
3 garlic cloves
1/2 teaspoon cumin seeds
1/4 teaspoon peppercorns
1 1/2 tomatoes
1 cup onion, cubed
1 green pepper, julienned
2 apples, chopped
1/3 cup raisins
2 teaspoons dried oregano
1 lime, cut into wedges
Salt
Pepper

Heat skillet and brown ground beef. Crush or grind garlic, cumin, and peppercorns. In a blender add spices, tomato and puree. Pour mixture over meat. Add onions and peppers and stir. Add apples, raisins and oregano and stir constantly. Simmer until juices are cooked off, but do not over cook meat. Drain fat and season to taste. Serve with warm tortillas and a twist of lime juice in each taco.

Serves 6

Roast With Peppers

6 pound chuck roast
4 garlic cloves
1 teaspoon cumin seeds
1/4 teaspoon black peppercorns
1 tablespoon butter
6 Anaheim peppers, chopped
2 onions, chopped
3/4 cup chicken broth
Salt
4 potatoes, sliced
4 carrots, sliced

Heat oven to 325 degrees. Crush or grind garlic, cumin and peppercorns to a smooth paste. Heat a skillet and add butter. Saute crushed spices, peppers and onions. Add broth and simmer. Season to taste. Heat a separate, dry, heavy skillet and sear the meat on high heat. Turn until it is thoroughly browned*. Set in an oven proof baking dish and pour saute mixture over roast. Cook for 1 1/2 to 2 hours checking on desired doneness.

*Set roast in a dutch oven and pour saute mixture over roast, potatoes, and carrots.

Serves 10

Spiced Sirloin

4 sirloin steaks
1 tablespoon olive oil
2 garlic cloves
1/4 teaspoon cumin seeds
1/4 teaspoon black peppercorns
2 tomatoes, diced
1/4 cup onion, chopped
1/8 teaspoon dried oregano
Salt

Crush or grind garlic, cumin and peppercorns. Heat skillet on high and add oil. Add all steaks and brown on both sides. Turn down the heat and cook steaks as desired. Salt to taste. Remove steaks and reserve steak juices. In the skillet with the reserve juices add the crushed spices and saute. Then add the tomatoes, onions and oregano. Simmer for 5 minutes and add the steaks. Bathe the steaks with the sauce for 2 minutes. Serve hot with vegetables of choice.

Serves 4

Steak Ranchero

Marinate:
1/2 teaspoon chili powder
2 tablespoons sugar
1/4 teaspoon ground black pepper
1/2 cup onion, diced
1 cup tomato, diced
2 serrano peppers, chopped
2/3 cup beer of choice
2 teaspoons lemon juice
2 teaspoons worcestershire sauce

Mix all ingredients together in a large bowl. Heat a skillet and add marinate. Boil and reduce to a simmer. Set aside and cool in a bowl.

4 shoulder steaks

Pierce each steak and set inside bowl with marinate and cover. Refrigerate for one hour or more. Grill steaks and reserve marinate. In a skillet, reheat marinate bringing it to a boil. Pour marinate over steaks. Serve hot.

Serves 4

Tampiquena Steak Dinner
Carne Tampiquena

2 ancho peppers
1 tomato, chopped
1/2 onion, chopped
1 garlic clove
1/4 teaspoon cumin seeds
1/8 teaspoon black peppercorns
6 corn tortillas

Heat a griddle on high and roast peppers until they are blackened on all sides. Place in a bowl of chilled water. Crush or grind garlic, cumin and peppercorns. Remove peppers from water and reserve water. Peel and de-vein peppers. In a blender add crushed spices, peppers, reserve water, tomatoes and onions. Puree until smooth. Heat a skillet and add sauce. Bring to a boil then pass each corn tortilla through sauce and fold. Remove and set aside. Keep warm.

6 breakfast steaks
6 lemons
Salt
Pepper
4 tablespoons cooking oil

Spread lemon juice, salt and pepper to taste on each steak. Heat skillet and add oil. Sear each steak and brown. Cook as desired. Breakfast steaks are very thin so they do not require a lot of cooking time. Set aside and keep warm.

2 avocados
Salt
Lettuce leaves
2 cups cooked refried beans
1 tomato, cut in slices
1/2 onion, cut in rings

In a bowl mash avocados and salt to taste. On each plate, place a breakfast steak, a folded tortilla dipped in sauce topped with onion rings, a tomato slice, a scoop of refried beans and a bed of lettuce leaves topped with mashed avocado. Enjoy!

Serves 6

Merida

Although Merida is a large city with a modern airport and nearly a million residents, it is still very much home to the Maya. I also found it to have the feeling of a small town.

At the central *zocalo*, the park is clean and children play freely while their parents or grandparents visit with friends. The *calesas* sit patiently at the corners waiting for a rider. Only in such a city as Merida could horse drawn carriages exist peacefully with motorized traffic.

At night, and on Sunday afternoon, people gather on one side of the *zocalo* to watch native performances that have captured some of what is left of Colonial Mexico.

The speciality of many local restaurants is a dish called *pibil*, which can include either pork, beef, or chicken. Regardless of the choice of meat, it features local spices and must be cooked in banana leaves to have that special Yucatan flavor.

The city of Merida is interesting in that at one time it had many millionaires due to the success of *henequen* growing on large plantations in the hinterland. A type of agave plant, it can be crushed and the remaining fiber made into ropes, rugs, and other products. The introduction of synthetic fibers has greatly diminished its demand, but the fabulous homes built by these Spanish and French *henequen barons* can still be seen on *Paseo de Montejo*, where many of the businessmen built their homes and administered their estates.

Few of the Europeans moved outside of the walled city of Merida during the Colonial period. The rural areas were still in rebellion and the Yucatan wasn't even recognized as a Mexican territory until 1936.

Beverages

Bloody Mary 1

1 1/2 ounces tequila
3 ounces tomato juice
1 tablespoon lemon juice
Dash worcestershire sauce
Dash hot sauce
Cracked ice
Salt
Pepper

Shake all ingredients with cracked ice. Strain into chilled glass.

Bloody Mary 2

1 1/2 ounces tequila
1 1/2 ounces tomato juice
1 tablespoon lemon juice
Cracked ice
Salt
Pepper

Shake all ingredients with cracked ice. Strain into chilled glass.

Cuba Libre

1 1/2 ounces white label rum
1 cola
Juice of 1/2 lime
Ice cubes

Fill a glass with ice and squeeze lime juice to cover. Pour rum and fill with cola.

Daiquiri

2 ounce white label rum
Juice of 1/2 lemon
1 teaspoon fine grain sugar

Shake all ingredients with cracked ice. Strain into chilled glass.

Frozen Daquiri

2 ounces white label rum
Juice of 1/2 lemon
1 teaspoon fine grain sugar
Dash of maraschino liqueur

In a blender add 8-10 ounces of cracked ice. Add all other ingredients and blend on high. Serve in a champagne glass.

Margarita

1 1/4 cups lemonade
1/4 cup freshly squeezed lime juice
1/8 teaspoon salt
1 cup tequila
1/3 cup Triple sec
Limes
Kosher salt
1 cup ice cubes
1 egg white

In a large pitcher mix lemonade, lime juice, salt, tequila and Triple sec. Stir well and refrigerate at least an hour. When drinks are ready to serve, rub the rims of the glasses with the limes and dip them in kosher salt. In a blender add the ice, egg white and contents of the pitcher. Blend on high until large chunks of ice have been crushed and the drink is frothy. Pour into glasses immediately.

Serves 4

Mexican Eggnog
Rompope

4 cups milk
1 cup sugar
1 cinnamon stick
1/4 teaspoon baking soda
12 egg yolks
1/2 cup brandy

In a saucepan add milk, sugar, cinnamon and baking soda. Bring to a boil and then lower flame and simmer for 15 minutes or until sugar has dissolved. Set aside and cool. In a large bowl beat the egg yolks until thick. Remove the cinnamon stick from the milk and slowly fold milk mixture into egg yolks. Keep beating mixture. Return the mixture to the saucepan and cook over low heat. Scrape bottom and side constantly. Do not overcook or you may end up with scrambled eggs. Let cool, then gradually stir in alcohol. Serve immediately

Yields: 1 quart

Screwdriver

2 ounces vodka
Orange juice
Ice cubes

In a 6 ounce glass add 3 ice cubes and vodka. Fill balance of glass with orange juice and stir.

Submarine
Submarino

1 shot glass of tequila
1 large mug of beer, 3/4 full

Drop the shot glass filled with tequila into the large mug of beer. Drink up!!

Te-Cola

1/2 lemon
1 ounce tequila
1 cola
Ice cubes

Fill a glass with ice and squeeze lemon juice to cover. Pour tequila and fill with cola.

Te-Collins

1 teaspoon sugar
1 tablespoon lemon juice
Ice cubes
1 ounce tequila
Club soda
Maraschino cherry

In a tall glass add sugar and lemon juice. Stir until it dissolves. Add ice and tequila and fill with club soda. Stir and top with cherry.

Te-Quini

2 ounces tequila
1 ounce dry vermouth
2 drops vanilla extract
Cracked ice

Shake all ingredients with cracked ice. Strain into chilled glass.

Tequila Sunrise

1 1/4 cups lemonade
1/4 cup freshly squeezed lime juice
1 cup tequila
4 tablespoons grenadine syrup
1 cup ice cubes
1 egg white

In a blender add all of the ingredients and blend on high until large chunks of ice have been crushed and the drink is frothy.   Pour into glasses immediately.

Tom Collins

2 ounces dry gin
1 tablespoon fine grain sugar
Juice of 1/2 lemon
Cola

Shake gin, sugar and lemon juice with cracked ice. Strain into chilled glass.   Add ice cubes and balance with cola.

Tequila Cocktail

2 ounces tequila
1 teaspoon fine grain sugar
Juice of 1/2 lime

Shake all ingredients with cracked ice. Strain into chilled glass.

Tequila

I have only visited the town of Tequila once, and my host was Mayor Eduardo Orendain, whose family is in the business of making Mexico's most famous beverage.

Tequila is made from the blue agave plant, which is cultivated on thousands of acres of land around the town of the same name. The area's unique soil composition contributes to the unique qualities of the agave plant and ultimately to the unique taste of the tequila.

Eduardo not only gave us a tour of the Orendain plant, which manufactures not only the family brand but also several contract labels as well. Later, he invited our party to his home, which has been in the family for generations.

An elaborate feast, which began with an array of appetizers, was offered. We ate and, of course, we drank. Endless family members toasted us with a bite and a shot of tequila.

By the time the main course arrived, my companions informed me that I was beginning to turn green. I excused myself and went to the restroom. When I looked in the mirror, I found that I had indeed been toasted one too many times.

Not long afterward, I was excused and we began the journey back to Guadalajara. I was very ill. Even today, the smell of Tequila (sorry Eduardo) makes me nauseas.

One friend in particular likes to point out that I'm the only person he's ever met who has tried to out drink the owners of a Tequila factory.

Breakfast

Breaded Breakfast Steak
Milanesa

6 breakfast steaks
2 eggs
2 cups bread crumbs
Oil
Salt
Pepper

Cut steak into serving size of choice or leave whole. In a large bowl beat eggs and season to taste. Put bread crumbs on a large plate. Pass each piece of steak in the egg mixture and then pat them into the bread crumbs. In a skillet heat oil and fry steaks as desired. These steaks are thin and do not require a long cooking time. Serve with a salad or beans.

Serves 6

Corn Tortillas With Eggs
Migas

3 tablespoons cooking oil
4 eggs
4 corn tortillas
Salt
Pepper

Cut corn tortillas in strips or triangles. In a bowl beat the eggs. Heat the skillet and add oil. Place the corn tortillas in the pan and saute, do not fry. Once the tortillas are pliable add the eggs and mix well. Season with salt and pepper. Serve with warm flour or corn tortillas and picante sauce.

Serves 2-4

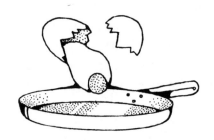

Corn Tortillas With Eggs Deluxe Migas

3 tablespoons cooking oil
4 eggs
1/4 cup onions
1/4 cup tomatoes, diced
4 corn tortillas
Salt
Pepper
Picante sauce (See recipe)

Cut corn tortillas in strips or triangles. In a bowl, beat the eggs. Heat the skillet and add oil. Place the corn tortillas, onions and tomatoes in the pan and saute, do not fry. Once the tortillas are pliable add the eggs and mix well. Season with salt and pepper. Serve with warm flour or corn tortillas and picante sauce.

Serves 2-4

Eggs With Shredded Beef
Huevos con Machacado

3 tablespoons cooking oil
4 eggs
1/4 cup onions
1/4 cup tomatoes, diced
1/2 cup machacado or 1 ounce beef jerky*
Salt
Pepper
1 cup hot sauce (See recipe)

In a bowl mix the eggs. Heat the skillet and add oil. Saute the onions and tomatoes. Add the meat and brown lightly on low heat. Add the eggs and mix well. Season with salt and pepper. Serve with warm flour or corn tortillas and hot sauce.

*Beef jerky should be heated under a broiler for 3 minutes. Cool then whirl in a blender. It should be about 1/2 a cup of thread-like meat fibers.

Serves 2-4

Ham And Eggs
Jamon y Huevos

2 eggs
1/2 cup of ham, cubed
1/4 cup onions, chopped
1/4 tomatoes, chopped
Salt
Pepper
Cooking oil

Heat skillet and add oil. In a bowl mix all ingredients well. Add to pan until the egg is cooked. Season to taste. Serve with hot flour or corn tortillas.

Serves 1-2

Mexican Sausage And Eggs
Chorizo y Huevos

3 eggs
1 link of Mexican sausage, *Chorizo*

Heat skillet and add sausage. Thoroughly cook sausage and brown on low heat. Add eggs to this and stir well until eggs are cooked. Serve with refried beans and tortillas.* Extra seasoning may not be necessary, since the sausage has quite a bit of salt.

Serves 2-4

Mexican Sausage And Refried Beans
Chorizo y Frijoles Refritos

1 cup of cooked pinto beans
1 link of Mexican sausage

Heat skillet and brown sausage thoroughly. Add beans in the same pan and stir occasionally for about five minutes. Mash beans and sausage until they are smooth. Serve with warm tortillas.

Serves 4

Potato And Egg Taquitos
Taquitos de Papas con Huevo

4 potatoes
3 eggs
Cooking oil
Salt
Pepper
Flour Tortillas
Optional:
Picante sauce

Wash, peel and dice potatoes. Heat skillet and add oil. Add the potatoes and cover. Stirring occasionally, fry until golden brown and uncover. Add the eggs and stir well to make sure all the eggs are cooked. Season to taste. Warm flour tortillas and add mixture in each tortilla.

Serves 4-6

Ranch-Style Eggs
Huevos Rancheros

Sauce:
2 tomatoes
Peppers of choice to taste
1/4 cup of onions, chopped
1 garlic clove, crushed

2 eggs
2 corn tortillas
Cooking oil
Salt
Pepper

To make the sauce, boil the tomatoes and then peel. Save the water. Puree all ingredients in a blender and add water from the reserve if needed.

Heat skillet and add oil. Pass each corn tortilla in the pan to soften, do not fry. Pat the tortillas for excess oil and stack them on a plate. Fry the eggs, "sunny-side up". Season to taste. Place the eggs on the tortillas and smother in sauce. Left over sauce can be refrigerated, if covered, for up to two days.

Serves 1-2

Red And Green Eggs
Huevos Rojos y Verdes

1 red tomato
1 serrano pepper

Boil together and puree in blender.

2 green tomatoes, *tomatillo*
1 jalapeno pepper

Simmer together and puree in blender. Do not let the tomatoes boil. If are punctured, they lose their flavor.

4 eggs
4 corn tortillas
Oil
Salt

Heat oil and pass tortillas through oil, do not fry. Set two tortillas side by side on each plate. Then fry eggs, sunny side up and place an egg on top of each tortilla. Pour red sauce on one egg and green sauce on the other egg.

Serves 2

Refried Beans And Egg
Frijoles Refritos con Huevos

1 cup refried beans, (See recipe)
2 eggs
Cooking oil
Optional:
Grated cheese of choice

Heat skillet and add oil. In a bowl mix eggs well
and add to pan. Cook eggs to desired consistency
and add the refried beans. Mix well and serve with
tortillas. Grated cheese may be added.

Serves 4

Guadalajara

Our plane tickets from Puerto Vallarta to
Guadalajara were in hand. We'd be on our way the
next morning. As I rested in the hotel room, I
turned the television set to CNN and discovered
that Guadalajara had blown up. The sewers had
exploded and literally thrown cars on top of
buildings.

More explosions were expected.

I went out to the jacuzzi where one of our
party was lounging with a drink.

"Guadalajara blew up."

"Right. I tried to call back to Texas and it was closed, too. Go away."

We took the flight the next morning anyway.

The Guadalajara airport was in bedlam. We were lucky enough to find a taxi, but we had to circle the city to get on the only street that was moving in or out of downtown. When we got to the hotel, the front desk couldn't find our reservations.

The city was locked down while everyone braced for another explosion and we had no room.

The next explosion never came and Guadalajara turned out to be a charming city that is attempting to recapture its colonial past. To be Mexico's second largest metropolitan area, the city is remarkably clean and well kept (except when the sewers explode).

For me, the area offered some of the most enjoyable shopping excursions in all of Mexico.

There is also a large colony of American and Canadian retirees who live around nearby Lake Chapala. Retirees are a real curiosity for most Mexicans because it is a foreign concept to them and this group of Americans, who don't have to work, contribute greatly to the perception that all Americans are rich.

Chicken

Chicken Fajitas
Fajitas de Pollo

Marinate:
4 chicken breasts, boneless and skinless
2 tablespoons olive oil
2 tablespoons fresh lime juice
1 red bell pepper, julienned
1 green bell pepper, julienned
1 onion, sliced in rings

Combine all ingredients in a large bowl and cover.
Refrigerate for two hours. Remove chicken breasts
and grill or bake as desired and save marinate.
Cut into strips. Heat a skillet and add marinate.
Saute lightly .

1 cup sharp cheddar cheese, grated
1 cup red sauce of choice
8 flour tortillas

Warm flour tortillas on a griddle or in the microwave. Fill each tortilla with chicken strips vegetables, cheese and sauce. Serve with rice and beans.

Serves 4

Chicken-Ka-Bobs

Ka-bob:
3 cups chicken cut in 2 inch cubes
Pearl onions, parboiled
Chunks green peppers, parboiled
Fresh mushrooms, lightly oiled
White rice, (See recipe)

Chicken Marinate:
4 garlic cloves
1/4 teaspoon cumin seeds
1/8 black peppercorns
1/2 cup fresh lemon juice
2 jalapeno peppers, chopped
2 tablespoons tomato paste
1 teaspoon dried oregano
1/4 teaspoon ground cinnamon

Crush or grind garlic, cumin seeds and peppercorns. In a shallow dish combine lemon juice, peppers, tomato paste, oregano, cinnamon and crushed spices. Place chicken chunks in marinate and cover. Turn occasionally while refrigerating for one hour. Remove chicken. On long skewers, thread the chicken and veggies in order of ingredients. Slide the skewers under the broiler. Broil or barbecue and turn frequently. Salt to taste. Serve with white rice.

Serves 4

Chicken In Mole Sauce-Shortcut Chicken Mole

1 whole chicken, sectioned
1 bay leaf
4 ounces of prepared mole

Boil chicken with bay leaf and save broth. In the blender add one cup of broth and mole and puree. Heat a skillet and add puree. Simmer on medium heat for 3 minutes and add chicken. Simmer for ten minutes and cover. Serve with rice and beans.

Serves 4

NOTE: Mole sauces are not something that a north-of-the-border cook is likely to tackle from scratch. This is a dark and heavy, thick sauce that includes such ingredients as dried chiles, nuts, seeds, vegetables, spices, and even a little chocolate. Tastes and preparations vary by region, but in each instance the mole sauce will virtually overwhelm the chicken or anything else it is served with. Mole is a native sauce that was in use in pre-Hispanic periods.

Chicken Quesadillas
Quesadillas de Pollo

1 pound chicken fajitas (See recipe)
6 ounces white cheese of choice
6 flour tortillas
1 cup lettuce, shredded
1 cup tomatoes, diced
1 cup guacamole (See recipe)
1 cup picante sauce

On medium to high heat, heat *comal* or griddle. Cut cheese in thin strips. Place one tortilla on the griddle and quickly place cheese strips to cover, add chicken strips and place a tortilla on top. Toast each side until golden brown or until cheese oozes out. Once cooked, put each quesadilla on a plate and cut in quarters and serve with condiments.

Serves 3

Chicken And Rice
Arroz con Pollo

2 garlic cloves
1/4 teaspoon cumin seeds
1/4 teaspoon black peppercorns
1 cup long grain rice
1/4 cup tomato sauce
1/2 chicken, sectioned *
3 tablespoons of oil
1/2 tomato, diced
1/4 cup onions, diced
1/4 cup bell pepper, julienned
2 cups water or chicken broth
Salt

Crush or grind garlic, cumin and peppercorns. Heat skillet and add oil. Add rice and brown. To this add tomato sauce and simmer for a minute. Add spices and vegetables and stir. Add water and chicken. Cover for twenty minutes on low heat or until the chicken is cooked. Season to taste. Serve with warm tortillas, beans and a meat of choice.

*1/2 pound of stew meat may be substituted

Serves 4-6

Chicken And Squash-Shortcut
Pollo con Calabaza

2 garlic cloves
1/4 teaspoon cumin seeds
1/4 teaspoon peppercorns
1whole chicken, sectioned
5 medium squash, sliced
1 can of whole kernel corn
1/4 cup onion, diced
1/4 cup tomatoes, diced
Salt
Pepper

Crush or grind garlic, cumin and peppercorns. Heat skillet and add oil. Lightly brown chicken and add all other ingredients including spices. The squash will release water, only 1/4 cup of water is needed. Cover and simmer. Keep from stirring frequently or it will turn to mush. Season to taste.

Serves 4

Chicken And Squash 2
Calabaza con Pollo

2 garlic cloves
1/4 teaspoon cumin seeds
1/4 teaspoon black peppercorns
1 whole chicken, skinned and sectioned
4 tablespoons cooking oil
1 tomato, diced
1/4 cup onions, diced
1/2 cup bell pepper, julienned
1/4 cup tomato sauce
1 cup water or chicken broth
1 can whole kernel corn
6 squash, sliced
Salt

Crush or grind garlic, cumin and peppercorns. Heat skillet and add oil. Add chicken and brown. To this add all other ingredients and stir. Cover for twenty minutes on low heat or until chicken is done. Season to taste. Serve with warm tortillas, beans and a meat of choice.

Serves 4

Chicken In Tomato Sauce
Pollo en Salsa

2 garlic cloves
1/4 teaspoon cumin seeds
1/4 teaspoon black peppercorns
1 whole chicken, sectioned
1 small onion, diced
1 cup tomato, diced
1/4 cup of bell pepper julienned
1 cup tomato sauce
1/4 cup water
1/4 cup cooking oil

Crush or grind garlic, cumin and peppercorns. Heat skillet and add oil. Lightly brown chicken. Add spices, tomatoes, tomato sauce, onions, bell peppers and water. Simmer for twenty minutes or until done. Season to taste. Serve with warm tortillas and beans.

Serves 4

Chicken Tortilla Crepes
Chimichangas de Pollo

1 chicken fryer, boiled
1 bay leaf
Cooking oil
2 garlic cloves
1/8 teaspoon cumin seeds
1/8 teaspoon peppercorns
1/4 cup onions
Salt
Lettuce, shredded
Tomato, diced
2 cups Monterrey Jack cheese, shredded
Sour Cream
Guacamole (See recipe)
Flour tortilla dough, see recipe of choice

Boil chicken with bay leaf. De-bone and shred chicken. Reserve the water. Crush garlic cloves, cumin seeds and peppercorns. Heat skillet and add oil. Saute chicken with spices. Season to taste. Add some chicken stock, then cook for a few minutes or until most of the juices are cooked off. Heat another skillet and add oil. Fold out tortillas and fill each with chicken then fold over and secure by pinching the sides together. Heat another skillet with 1/4 inch of oil and fry chimichangas until golden brown on both sides. Top with lettuce, tomato, cheese, sour cream and guacamole.

Serves 8-10

Chicken Wings With Chickpeas
Pollo con Garbanzos

6 chicken wings
1 bay leaf
2 cans chickpeas
1 tomato
1/2 onion
1 garlic clove
1/4 teaspoon cumin seeds
1/8 teaspoon peppercorns
2 tablespoons cooking oil
Salt

Boil wings with bay leaf and reserve water. If desired remove chickpea shells. In a small pot, boil tomato. Crush or grind garlic, cumin and pepper corns with tomato. This will make a spicy tomato sauce. Heat skillet and add oil and tomato sauce. If a gravy is desired add one tablespoon of flour and brown. Then add chicken wings and chick peas. Add 1/4 cup or more of reserve water. Simmer and stir. Season to taste. Serve warm with corn tortillas and white rice.

Serves 4

Pearl Chicken
Pollo con Cebollitas

1 chicken fryer, sectioned
4 bacon slices, chopped
10 pearl onions
1/4 cup vinegar
1 cup chicken broth
1/4 cup coriander leaves, chopped
Cooking Oil
Salt
Pepper

Heat skillet and fry bacon. Add chicken pieces and onions. Saute lightly. If there is too much grease, drain as desired. Add vinegar, water and coriander. Cover and simmer until chicken is cooked and tender. Season to taste. Serve hot with vegetable of choice.

Serves 4

Pepper Chicken Breasts

2 garlic cloves
1/4 teaspoon cumin seeds
1/4 teaspoon black peppercorns
1/4 cup onion, diced
1/4 green bell pepper, julienned
1/4 red bell pepper, julienned
1/4 cup diced celery
1/4 cup mushrooms, sliced
1 Habanero pepper, chopped
1/8 teaspoon cayenne pepper
1 cup chicken stock
1 lime
1 teaspoons cornstarch
2 teaspoons cooking sherry
4 chicken breasts
Flour
1 cup olive oil

Crush or grind garlic, cumin and peppercorns. Heat a skillet and add 3 tablespoons of the oil. Saute crushed spices, onions, bell peppers, celery, mushrooms, Haberano, and cayenne for about 5 minutes. Add the chicken, stock and squeeze the lime into the pan. Bring to a boil. In a bowl add the cornstarch and the sherry and mix well. Add this mixture to the pan and continue to simmer. Remove this pan from heat and set aside. Roll chicken breasts in flour. Heat another skillet and add olive oil to cover the bottom. Fry chicken on both sides until they brown. Remove and drain on paper toweling. Heat skillet with saute to a simmer, then add the chicken breasts. Stir constantly until thickened. Serve with white rice (See recipe).

Serves 4

Moctezuma's Temple

When we visited the ruins of the pre-Hispanic Totonac village of Zempoala, we were overcome with a sense of history. There we were, standing at the very site where the Totonac chief, who Cortes nicknamed "the fat cacique," offered a bribe to the Spanish to protect his people from the Aztec.

It was during these discussions with the Totonacs that Aztec tax collectors arrived and demanded twenty individuals for use in sacrificial rituals. Cortes objected and took the Aztec captive.

Cortes wanted to Christianize the Totonacs, but after several days of witnessing human sacrifice being performed by the Aztec at Moctezuma's Temple, conversion seemed improbable. About fifty Spaniards attacked the temple and destroyed the pagan idols inside.

We wanted to see Moctezuma's Temple, but there are no signs marking the various structures at Zempoala and our guide was unfamiliar with the site. As we drove around the area in the van, we kept the side door open so we could ask everyone we met where to find the temple.

Our search took us to a dirt road in a sugar cane field. It appeared to me that we were lost, but we stopped a family on the trail who had a few days supply of wood for the stove tied to the back of a burro. They pointed ahead to a dusty path that led into the cane field. About seventy-five yards up the narrow path we came to the remains of a small pyramid, which was guarded by a rusting and unlocked chain link fence.

Thus, we found Moctezuma's Temple. If it were located in the U.S., there would be an acre of asphalt around it rather than sugar cane and you'd have to pay the park commission six figures each year in concession fees to open a hot dog stand.

Desserts

Anise Cookies

4 eggs
1 pound confectioners' sugar
1 teaspoon baking powder
2 teaspoons aniseed
Rind of one lemon, grated
1 cup almonds, finely chopped
1/8 teaspoon salt
2 cups flour, sifted

Heat oven to 400 degrees. In a large bowl beat eggs. Sift sugar with the baking powder and add to eggs, beating well. Add aniseed, lemon rind and almonds. Stir well. Add salt to the sifted flour. Add this to the other ingredients. Mix until batter has stiffened. Grease a cookie sheet and drop teaspoonfuls of mixture. Bake for 8-10 minutes.

Yields: 5 dozens cookies

Avacodo-Lime Sorbet

2/3 cup sugar
2/3 cup water
2 large ripe avocados, peeled and pureed
1/4 cup fresh lime juice
Dash of hot pepper
Pinch of salt

In a small saucepan combine sugar and water over medium heat. Stir until sugar is dissolved. Just before mixture comes to a boil, remove from heat. Cool, then cover and chill. Beat avocado with lime juice until completely smooth. Add pepper sauce and salt and blend well. Chill. Stir in syrup. Finish in freezer or in cream maker.

Yields: 3 cups

Blueberry Delight

6 cups fresh blueberries
1/3 cup sugar
1 teaspoon vanilla
1 teaspoon grated lemon peel

In a bowl mix all ingredients gently. Cover and chill overnight.

Yields: 6 cups

Bread and Honey Dessert

4 slices of white bread
1/2 cup milk
1 egg, lightly beaten
2 tablespoons butter
1/4 cup clear honey
1/4 cup dry sherry

Heat oven to 325 degrees. Remove bread crusts and cut into large strips. Arrange the bread on a shallow dish and pour the milk over the bread. Let it soak for 5 minutes. Drain excess milk. Take the bread out and dip into egg and set aside. Heat a skillet and add butter. Fry bread pieces until golden brown and set aside. In a bowl add honey and sherry. Mix well. In an oven-proof dish, place the bread and pour honey mixture over. Bake for 25 minutes until golden brown. Remove from pan and serve immediately.

Serves 2

Isla Mujeres

What would a Caribbean Island be without tales of romance and adventure? Off the coast of Cancun is *Isla Mujeres*, which has its own legends of love, both lost and found.

When I was there, the *Hacienda Mundaca*, which sits in ruins near the south end of the Island, was being rebuilt. According to local lore, the estate was built by Fermin Mundaca de Marehaja, a retired pirate and slave trader who wanted to impress a local lady enough that she would consent to marry him.

Alas, despite his lavish wealth, she refused and married another. Mundaca is said to have lived the remainder of his life a broken man.

(I found out later on when we visited the *El Garrafon* National Park that the two twenty-foot plus snakes they had on display were captured on the Mundaca property. If I had known there were snakes that large at the Hacienda, I would have taken a short visual tour from the front seat of the car instead of on foot.)

At the most southern tip of *Isla Mujeres* are the only remaining Maya ruins on the island. They were built to embody fertility and honor the goddess of the moon. It is believed that the Maya women gathered there to pray prior to their marriage in order to be blessed with many children. It is from this practice that *Isla Mujeres*, or Island of Women, gets its name.

Our guide told us that at one time there were many more idols on the site, but that Hernan Cortes had personally ordered them destroyed.

Caramelized Mexican Candy
Leche Quemada

2 large cans evaporated milk
5 1/2 cups sugar
5 1/2 tablespoons butter
1 teaspoon salt
1/2 brown sugar

In a large saucepan mix in milk, sugar, butter and salt and bring to a boil. Add brown sugar and stir until it dissolves in the mixture. Stir constantly until the mixture thickens. Butter a baking dish and pour mixture. Let cool and cut into squares and serve.

Yields: 3 dozen

Carrot Cake

2 cups sugar
3 cups flour
2 teaspoons cinnamon
1 teaspoon baking soda
1 1/2 cups oil
1/2 cup buttermilk
4 eggs
1 cup pecans
3 cups finely grated carrots

Heat oven to 300 degrees. In a large bowl, sift dry ingredients together. To this add oil, buttermilk, and eggs. Beat well. Mix in pecans and carrots. Grease and flour tube pan. Pour mixture into pan and bake for 1 1/2 hours or until a toothpick which has been inserted comes out clean. Let cool on cake rack and then spread icing.

Icing:

1-8 ounce package cream cheese
1 stick butter or margarine
1 cup shredded coconut
2 teaspoons vanilla extract
1 pound confectioners sugar
1/2 cup pecans

In a large bowl, cream together cheese and butter. Add coconut, vanilla, sugar and pecans. Mix well and spread on carrot cake.

Chocolate Almond Cookies
Galletas de Chocolate y Almendras

1/2 cup or stick butter
1/2 cup sugar
1 tablespoon flour
1/4 teaspoon salt
3/4 ground blanched almonds
2 tablespoons milk
1 teaspoon almond extract
3 1/2 ounces semi-sweet chocolate, melted

Heat oven to 350 degrees. Line baking sheets with foil, then butter and flour baking sheets. Heat a saucepan and melt butter on medium heat. To this add sugar, flour and salt. Stir until sugar dissolves. Mix in almonds and milk. Once it thickens, remove from heat and add almond extract. Stir and let cool slightly. Drop a spoonful of mixture on the baking sheet. Space about 3 inches apart. Bake 5-7 minutes or until golden brown. Let cool then remove. Bake one cookie sheet at a time. Cover one side of cookie with melted chocolate. Cool until chocolate sets.

Yields: 2 dozen cookies

Coffee Flan
Flan de Cafe

1/2 cup +2 tablespoons sugar
2 cups milk
1 tablespoon instant coffee powder
2 eggs
2 egg yolks
1 cup heavy cream

In a wide pan, melt 1/2 cup of sugar until it is golden brown caramel. Pour into a warmed 1 quart baking dish. Cover bottom with caramelized mixture by tilting pan. Set aside. Heat oven to 350 degrees. In a saucepan, scald the milk and stir in coffee powder until it is dissolved. Lightly beat the eggs and the egg yolks with the 2 tablespoons of sugar until the sugar has dissolved. Stir in the hot milk and the cream. Strain this on top of the caramelized mixture.

Place the dish in a roasting pan and pour enough boiling water into the sauce pan to come about one inch up the sides of the dish. Bake for one hour or until the flan sets. Test by inserting a knife in the center, it comes out clean. Let cool and then chill.

Serves 10

Gelatin Surprise

1 14 ounce can of cubed pineapples
2 small boxes of gelatin
1 pint cottage cheese
1 pint cool whip

Drain pineapples and reserve liquid. In a sauce pan add pineapple juice reserve and gelatin. Simmer on low heat until it dissolves. Let it cool about twenty minutes. Mix pineapples, cottage cheese and cool whip. To this mixture, gently stir in gelatin. Refrigerate until mixture thickens. Serve chilled. Great for children's parties.

Serves 6

Flamed Bananas
Platanos Flameados

4 large ripe bananas, peeled
2 tablespoons butter
1/2 cup light brown sugar
1/4 cup orange juice
1/2 cup rum

Combine the butter, sugar and orange juice. Heat skillet and melt this mixture until smooth. Cut bananas lengthwise. Add them to the pan and cook gently. Turn frequently until they are hot and softened, but not mushy.

Add the rum and warm it briefly. Set a light and spoon the flaming sauce over the bananas until the flames die out. Serve immediately.

Serves 4

Iced-Mango Dessert

4 ripe mangos
1/2 cup water
2 tablespoons honey
2 tablespoons fresh lemon juice

Cut mangoes in half. In a blender, spoon all the mango pulp in it as possible. Puree until smooth. Set aside. In a small saucepan, combine water and honey. Bring to boil over medium heat, stirring occasionally to dissolve honey. Reduce heat and simmer 5 minutes. Remove from heat and cool. To mango puree add lemon juice and honey mixture. Blend well. Pour into ice cube tray and freeze until firm or about 3 hours. Before serving let soften, slightly.

Yields: 3 cups

Mexican Pillows
Sopaipillas

2 cups flour
1/2 teaspoon baking powder
1 1/2 teaspoon salt
1/2 teaspoon sugar
1 1/2 teaspoon vegetable oil
1 tablespoon evaporated milk
1/8 cup warm water
Oil for frying
Honey
1/2 cup powdered sugar

In a large bowl mix flour, baking powder, salt, and sugar. Then add oil, milk, and water. Knead on a floured surface, until dough forms. Cover with a plastic bag and let it sit for 1/2 hour. Then separate into small balls and roll out as thin as possible. Cut into squares or triangles. Heat oil for deep frying. Bathe sopaipillas with hot oil so they can puff up. Serve hot topped with honey and or sprinkled powdered sugar. Sopaipillas are best eaten hot and freshly made. These should not be served cold or reheated.

Yield: 3 dozen sopaipillas

Mexican Wedding Cookies 1
Galletas de Boda

1 cup butter or margarine
2 cups flour
1/4 cup powdered sugar
1 teaspoon baking powder
3 teaspoons vanilla
1 cup pecans, finely chopped
Powdered sugar, to roll cookies

In a bowl whip butter until light and fluffy. In another mixing bowl add flour, sugar and baking powder. Sift these ingredients well. Add this dry mixture to the butter. Then add vanilla and pecans. Mix well. Heat oven to 350 degrees. On an ungreased baking sheet, drop a teaspoonful of mixture or shape into crescents with fingers. Bake cookies for 10 minutes or until brown. Roll cookies in powdered sugar while hot.

Yields: 4 dozen cookies

Mexican Wedding Cookies 2
Galletas de Boda

1/2 cup or 1 stick unsalted butter, at room
temperature
1 cup flour
1/2 cup sifted powdered sugar
1/2 cup finely chopped pecans or almonds
1/2 teaspoon vanilla
Pinch of salt
Powdered sugar

Heat oven to 350. In a bowl beat butter until light
and fluffy. Add flour, 1/4 cup of sugar, nuts,
vanilla and salt. Continue beating until it forms a
soft dough. Wrap tightly and freeze for 1 hour.
Dough should be firm enough to pinch off small
pieces. Take the dough and roll back and forth in
your hands and form into crescents. Place them
on an ungreased baking sheet about 1 1/2 apart.
Place in the center of oven and bake until golden
brown. While still warm, roll in powdered sugar.

Yields: 1 dozen cookies

Nut Cookies
Galletas de Nuez

2 eggs
1 cup light brown sugar
1 cup chopped nuts
Pinch of salt
6 tablespoons flour

Heat oven to 350 degrees. Separate eggs in one bowl and beat egg yolk until they are thick. Gradually beat in sugar and add the nuts and salt. In another bowl beat egg whites until they are stiff. Fold them into the first mixture then stir in the flour. On an ungreased cookie sheet, drop a spoon full of mixture, leaving about 2 inches between them to spread. Flatten with a knife and bake for 5 minutes or until done.

Yields: 4 dozen cookies

Pecan Candy

4 cups sugar
2 cups milk
1 tablespoon butter
1 teaspoon vanilla
2 cups pecan halves

In a heavy sauce pan brown 1 cup of sugar, until it is caramelized. In another pan add the rest of the sugar and milk. When this mixture comes to a boil, slowly add the caramelized sugar. Continue to boil until mixture thickens, then add the butter and vanilla. Stir well, then drop spoonfuls on waxed paper topping with a pecan half.

Yields: 3 dozen

Pecan Clusters

1/4 cup butter
1/2 cup sugar
1 egg
1 1/2 teaspoon vanilla extract
2 squares unsweetened chocolate, melted
1/2 cup sifted flour
1/4 teaspoon baking powder
1/2 teaspoon salt
2 cups pecans, chopped

Heat oven to 325 degrees. In a bowl cream together butter and sugar. To this add egg and vanilla and mix well. Add chocolate and dry ingredients. Stir in pecans. Grease a baking sheet and drop teaspoonfuls of mixture. Bake for 8-10 minutes.

Yields: 2 dozen clusters

Peanut Brittle

3 cups sugar
1/2 cup water
1 cup light corn syrup
3 cups raw peanuts
1 tablespoon baking soda
1/4 cup butter
1 teaspoon vanilla

In a heavy saucepan add sugar, water and corn syrup. On medium heat (without boiling) cook this mixture until sugar dissolves, then add peanuts. Now bring to a boil and stir gently until golden brown. Checking with a candy thermometer, the temperature should reach 300 degrees. You can also check the candy by dropping a drop of the candy mixture in ice water. If it turns hard, it is ready. The peanuts will start popping. Remove saucepan from the heat and add baking soda, butter and vanilla and stir until the butter melts and the mixture starts to foam. Pour immediately into 2 butter jelly roll pans and spread out with a spatula. Butter your fingers and when the mixture starts to harden and cool, stretch it as thin as possible with your fingers. Once it completely hardens, crack it into desired pieces.

Yields: 3 1/2 cups

Rice Pudding
Atole de Arroz

1/2 cup white rice
2 cups water
1 cinnamon stick
1/2 cup evaporated milk
1/4 tablespoon salt
1/2 cup sugar
1/4 teaspoon vanilla
Ground cinnamon

Optional:
Raisins

Bring the water to a boil with the cinnamon sticks for five minutes. Pour in the rice and let it boil for twenty minutes. Stir once, until the liquid is cooled and the rice is tender. Add all other ingredients. Stir and simmer another fifteen minutes. Do not overcook. Stir gently. Sprinkle each bowl with ground cinnamon and raisins if desired.

Serves 4

Spiced Apples With Vanilla Ice Cream
Nieve de Vainilla con Manzanas

3 large apples, sliced thin
2 tablespoons canola oil
1/2 cup cranberry juice
1 tablespoon honey
1/4 teaspoon ground cinnamon
1/8 teaspoon ground allspice
1/8 teaspoon grated nutmeg
1/2 gallon vanilla ice cream

Heat a large skillet and add oil. Saute apples until tender, but not too mushy. Remove and keep warm. In a separate pan add juice, honey, cinnamon, allspice and nutmeg. Cover and cook on medium heat until mixture is syrupy. Add apples to mixture and heat for 1 minute. Cover apples with glaze. Serve each plate with glazed apples and 2 scoops of ice cream.

Serves 4

Spice Cake

1/4 pound butter
1 cup sugar
1/2 cup dark-brown sugar
4 eggs
1/2 cup milk
1/2 cup molasses
2 1/2 cups flour
1 teaspoon salt
1/2 teaspoon baking soda
2 teaspoons cinnamon
1/2 teaspoon cloves
1/4 teaspoon nutmeg
1/8 teaspoon cayenne pepper
Optional:
Frosting, see below

Heat oven to 350 degrees. Butter and lightly flour an 8 inch square pan. In a large bowl, cream the butter, slowly adding the two sugars. Beat until light and fluffy. Beat in the eggs and then add the milk and molasses. Beat thoroughly. In a separate bowl, mix the rest of the ingredients together. Add to the first mixture and beat well. Pour batter into the pan and bake about 45 minutes. Test with a toothpick in the center until it comes out clean. Let cool and frost if desired.

Frosting:
1/4 pound butter
1/2 cup dark brown sugar
1/4 milk
2 cups powdered sugar

In a heavy sauce pan melt butter and brown sugar stirring over medium heat. Add milk and stir. Let cool, then beat in the powdered sugar until thick enough to spread.

Serves 10

Sponge Cake

6 eggs separated
1 teaspoon cream of tartar
1 1/2 cup sugar
1 1/4 cup sifted flour
1/2 teaspoon baking powder
Salt
1 1/4 teaspoon vanilla extract
1/4 cup butter
1/4 cup shortening
3 cups sifted powdered sugar
1-8.5 ounce can crushed pineapple, drained
1/2 teaspoon grated lemon rind

In a large bowl, beat egg whites with cream of tartar. Add 1/2 cup sugar gradually, beating until stiff. In a small mixer bowl, sift flour, 1 cup sugar, baking powder and 1/2 teaspoon salt together. To these dry, sifted ingredients add: egg yolks, 1/4 cup of water and 1 teaspoon vanilla. Beat on medium speed until light and fluffy. Fold this mixture into stiffly beaten egg whites. Pour into an ungreased, 10-inch tube pan. Bake at 350 degrees for 45 minutes. Invert on cake rack and cool. In a bowl cream butter and shortening adding powdered sugar gradually. Beat until light and fluffy. Stir in remaining ingredients with 1/8 teaspoon salt and 1/4 teaspoon vanilla. Spread on cooled cake.

Serves 16

Acapulco

The most famous tourist destination in Mexico is Acapulco, which is located on the Pacific Coast and features what are probably the world's most photographed beaches.

Acapulco has had an international flavor since colonial times, when pirate ships called this deep nature harbor home base for their marauding of the Spanish fleet that traded with Manilla in the Philippines and in Asia.

The Spanish ships carried millions of dollars worth of cargo, even in modern currency. They normally returned from the East during the first week of December and a great festival would be held. That celebration continues today, only it is now called the Our Lady of Guadelupe Festival.

I have found this annual event to be one of my personal favorites.

Vendors set up on the *zocalo*, or main square, near the harbor, and circle the blue and yellow twin-domed Acapulco Cathedral. Children wear the traditional cotton clothing and attend mass with their extended families that often include grandparents and even great grandparents. Afterward, they are treated to sugar cookies, roasted corn on a stick, or some other available delight.

Although most of us remember Acapulco for its glitz and glamour, its world class night life, *La*

Quebrada divers, or the rich and famous who frequent its beaches, I think I like it best for the romance of its rich history and the native people who were boat builders, fishermen, and sailors long before the tourists came and high rise hotels and condominiums captured the skyline.

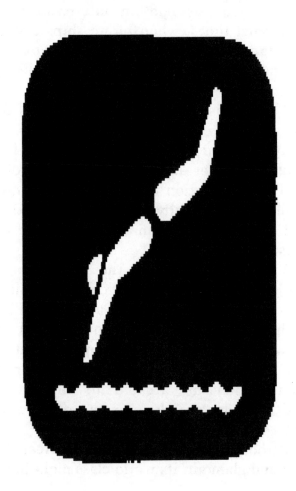

Dips & Sauces

Avocado Cream Dip

1 cup sour cream
1/2 cup green chillies, drained and chopped
1 avocado, peeled and cubed
1/8 teaspoon cayenne pepper
1/4 teaspoon garlic powder
1/4 teaspoon onion powder
Salt

In a bowl, mix all ingredients. Do not crush avocado. Season to taste. Chill and serve with corn tortilla chips.

Serves 6

Avocado Dip
Guacamole

4 avocados
1 tomato, diced
1 tablespoon of lemon juice
Salt

Cut open avocados and save seeds. Spoon out the fruit and blend in a bowl until creamy. Add lemon juice and salt to taste. Mix in the tomatoes and serve chilled with corn tortilla chips as an appetizer.

Serves 4

Bean Dip

2 tablespoons vegetable oil
1 garlic clove, crushed
1/4 red onion, chopped
1 jalapeno pepper, stemmed and chopped
2 cups red kidney bean puree or refried pinto beans, see recipe
2 tablespoons chili powder
1/2 teaspoon oregano, chopped fresh

Heat skillet and add oil. Saute garlic, onion and pepper. Add this mixture and all other ingredients in a blender. Blend on high until smooth. Return mixture to pan and heat thoroughly. Serve warm with flour or corn tortilla chips.

Yields: 3 cups

Cooked Green Hot Sauce 1
Chile Guisadao

1/2 tomato, diced
3 tablespoons onions, diced
2 jalapeno or serrano peppers, diced
1 tablespoon olive oil
1/4 cup water or chicken broth
1 tablespoon coriander leaves, chopped
Salt

Heat skillet and add oil. Saute onion until soft. Remove from heat. In a blender, add the rest of the ingredients and puree. Pour this into the skillet and return to heat. Season to taste. Simmer for five minutes. Serve with warm corn tortillas.

Serves 2

Cooked Green Hot Sauce 2
Chile Guisadao

3 tablespoons olive oil
1 tomato, diced
1/2 cup onions, diced
2 jalapeno peppers, diced
2 serrano peppers, diced
1 cup chicken stock
1 garlic clove, chopped
2 tablespoons coriander leaves, chopped
Salt

Heat skillet and add oil. Saute onion and garlic. Then stir in stock. Remove from heat. In a blender add the rest of the ingredients and puree. Pour this into the skillet and return to heat. Season to taste. Simmer for five minutes. Serve with warm corn tortillas.

Serves 2

Jalapa

The best coffee in Mexico is grown in the state of Veracruz. Thousands of acres of coffee and bananas exist near Jalapa, the capital of the state, which is located inland in what has often been described as Mexico's "Garden of Eden."

Sitting at about 4,000 feet above sea level, the region offers a subtropical climate with an average temperature of 66 degrees. It is among the most comfortable and pleasant areas in the entire country.

One of the most attractive towns is Coatepec, a Totonac village which sits within sight of Orizaba, a landmark, snowcapped mountain of 18,500 feet that overlooks this town, Jalapa, Xico, and many others. The greater the elevation at which the coffee is grown, the better the taste. Sadly, when I was last in Coatepec, the price of coffee beans was so low that the plantation owners could not even afford to pay for them to be harvested. The beans that were not taken for local consumption simply fell to the ground and rotted. The market for bananas was not much better and much of what was harvested was being fed to livestock.

About seven miles from Coatepec is another Totonac village, named Xico, which is best known within the region for its bakeries, mole dishes, and local liquors.

Of course, the best known food product of the region is the Jalapeno pepper, which obtained its name from the city of Jalapa.

If traveling in the region, a visitor should plan to spend at least half a day at Jalapa's Museum of Anthropology, which offers a world class display of pre-Hispanic artifacts. I would suggest that you purchase a museum tour book at the front desk, which is available in English.

Cream Cheese Dip

1/2 pound light softened cream cheese
2 garlic cloves
1/4 teaspoon black peppercorns
1 lime
2 tablespoons coriander leaves, chopped
2 tablespoons parsley leaves, chopped
3 tablespoons chives, chopped
1/2 teaspoon thyme
Salt

Crush or grind garlic and peppercorns with lime juice. In a mixing bowl blend all other ingredients well. Season to taste. Refrigerate and cover until ready to serve. Serve with flour tortilla chips or raw vegetables like: celery or carrots.

Serves 4-6

Garden Fresh Picante 1
Pico De Gallo

1 tomato, diced
1 onion, diced
1 serrano pepper, chopped
1/2 cup fresh coriander leaves
1 lemon

In a bowl mix tomato, onion, pepper and coriander. Squeeze lemon juice and stir. Natural juices are released and no water needs to be added. Chill for 1 hour to let flavors blend. Serve with corn tortilla chips.

Yields: 2 cups

Garden Fresh Picante 2
Pico De Gallo

1 tomato, diced
1 onion, diced
1 avocado, peeled and diced
1 serrano pepper, chopped
1/2 cup fresh coriander leaves
1 lemon
1 teaspoon olive oil

In a bowl mix tomato, onion, avocado, pepper and coriander. Squeeze lemon juice and add oil. Toss gently. Natural juices are released and no water needs to be added. Chill for 1 hour to let flavors blend. Serve with corn tortilla chips.

Yields: 2 cups

NOTE: Many of the recipes presented in this book require the grinding together of ingredients in a mortar and pestle, or *molcajete* and *tejolote*. The ones sold in Mexico are made from black basalt, a volcanic rock. Many families pass these utensils generation to generation as a heirloom.

Green Sauce-Mild
Salsa Verde

10 green tomatoes, *tomatillos*
2 jalapeno or serrano peppers
1 slice of bread
1 small banana
1/4 garlic clove
Coriander sprigs to taste
Salt

First, peel the brown casing on the *tomatillos*.
Simmer tomatoes and peppers in the same pot for
ten minutes. Do not let them boil or they will split
and lose their flavor. In a blender, puree tomatoes,
peppers, bread, banana, garlic and coriander.
Season to taste. Serve with chips or a meal.

Yields 2 pints

Green Sauce-Medium
Salsa Verde

10 green tomatoes, *tomatillos*
4 jalapeno or serrano peppers
1 slice of bread
1 small banana
1/4 garlic clove
Coriander sprigs to taste
Salt

First, peel the brown casing on the *tomatillos*. Simmer tomatoes and peppers in the same pot for ten minutes. Do not let them boil or they will split and lose their taste. In a blender, puree tomatoes, peppers, bread, banana, garlic and coriander. Season to taste. Serve with chips or a meal.

Yields 2 pints

NOTE: *Tomatillos*, or Mexican Green Tomatoes, are not tomatoes at all, but are a member of the gooseberry family of plants. Fresh *tomatillos* are not always available in many parts of the United States, but they are sold in cans. This fruit is used in many of the green sauces associated with Mexican cooking.

Green Sauce-Hot
Salsa Verde

10 green tomatoes, *tomatillos*
6 jalapeno or serrano peppers
1 slice of bread
1 small banana
1/4 garlic clove
Coriander sprigs to taste
Salt

First, peel the brown casing on the *tomatillos*. Simmer tomatoes and peppers in the same pot for ten minutes. Do not let them boil or they will split and lose their flavor. In a blender, puree tomatoes, pepper, bread, banana, garlic and coriander. Season to taste. Serve with chips or a meal.

Yields 2 pints

Green Sauce

4 ounce can green chilies, drained
3 pickled jalapeno peppers
3 tablespoons scallions, chopped
2 tablespoons coriander leaves, chopped
2 tablespoons fresh lime juice
1/2 teaspoon dried oregano
1/4 teaspoon ground cumin
Salt
Pepper

In a blender puree all ingredients. Pour in a bowl.
Chill until ready to serve.

Yields: 2/3 cup

Hot Sauce With Cheese 1
Salsa de Chile Con Queso

2 tablespoons butter
2 tomatoes, chopped
1 onion, chopped
4 serrano peppers, julienned
8 ounces Monterrey Jack cheese, cubed
Salt
Pepper

Heat skillet and add butter. Saute onion and tomato. Add peppers and cheese cubes. Simmer until cheese melts. Season to taste. Serve with corn tortillas, chips, eggs or a meal.

Serves 6

Hot Sauce With Cheese 2
Salsa de Chile Con Queso

2 tablespoons butter
2 tomatoes, chopped
1 onion, chopped
4 serrano peppers, julienned
2 tablespoons coriander leaves, chopped
1 garlic clove, minced
8 ounces Monterrey Jack cheese, cubed
Salt
Pepper

Heat skillet and add butter. Saute onion, tomato, coriander, peppers and garlic. Add cheese cubes. Simmer until cheese melts. Season to taste. Serve with corn tortillas, chips, eggs or a meal.

Serves 4-6

Hot Sauce With Cheese 3
Chile con Queso

2 tomatoes, diced
1 onion, diced
4 jalapeno peppers, julienned
2 tablespoons butter
4 cups American cheese, cubed
1/4 cup milk

Heat a skillet and add butter. Saute tomatoes, onion and peppers. Then add cheese and milk. Stir on medium heat until melted . Serve hot with corn tortilla chips.

Serves 6

Hot Sauce With Lemon
Chile con Lemon

6 lemons
6 Jap peppers or *chile Japones*

In a blender squeeze all lemons. Then add peppers. Blend and puree. Serve chilled with corn chips or fajita tacos. This sauce is very hot!!

Yields: 1 cup

Hot Sauce With Limes
Chile con Limas

4 limes
2 habanero peppers, chopped
1 purple onion, diced
1 tomato, diced

In a blender squeeze all limes. Then add peppers, onions and tomato. Blend and puree. This sauce can be tossed and served without being pureed. Serve chilled with corn chips. This sauce is extremely hot!!

Yields: 3/4 cup

NOTE: The habanero pepper is the only variety grown on the Yucatan peninsula that has no Mayan name and some researchers feel it was first brought to Mexico from Cuba by the Spanish. One thing is certain, the habanero is the hottest of the hot. I would suggest that you wear gloves when handling it.

Red Sauce-Mild
Salsa

2 tomatoes
1 jalapeno or serrano pepper
Salt

Boil tomatoes and peppers in the same pot for ten minutes. In a blender, puree tomatoes and pepper. Season to taste. Serve with chips or a meal.

Yields: 1 pint

Red Sauce-Medium
Salsa

2 tomatoes
2 jalapeno or serrano peppers
1/4 clove of garlic
Salt

Boil tomatoes and peppers in the same pot for ten minutes. In a blender, puree tomatoes, peppers and garlic. Season to taste. Serve with chips or a meal.

Yields: 1 pint

Red Sauce-Hot
Salsa

2 tomatoes
3 jalapeno or serrano peppers
1 clove of garlic
1/8 teaspoon black peppercorns
Salt

Boil tomatoes and peppers in the same pot for ten minutes. In a blender, puree tomatoes, peppers,. garlic and peppercorns. Season to taste. Serve with chips or a meal.

Yields: 1 pint

Red Sauce For Enchiladas
Salsa Roja Para Enchiladas

3 tablespoons chili powder
3 tablespoons flour
1 cup stewed tomatoes
3 tablespoons oil
2 cups water
3/4 teaspoon salt

Heat skillet and add oil. Stir in flour and brown. Stir in salt and chili powder. Remove from heat and add tomatoes and water. Place on heat and continue to simmer for 15 minutes.

Yields: 3 cups

Red Sauce For Stews
Salsa Roja Para Caldillos

4-6 dried red ancho peppers
2 cups water

Remove stems and seeds from peppers. In a sauce pan, place peppers and cover with water. Bring to boil and simmer for 15 minutes. Set aside and cover for one hour. Puree in blender. This sauce can be warmed and served with meat or mixed in with cheese to make an enchilada sauce.

Yields: 2 cups

Spicy Dip

1 pint sour cream
1 tablespoon lemon juice
1 tablespoon worcestershire sauce
2 teaspoons minced onions
1 1/2 teaspoons celery salt
1/4 teaspoon garlic powder
1/4 teaspoon Tabasco sauce

In a bowl mix all ingredients well. Chill for at least 1 hour. Serve with chips or raw vegetables.

Yields: 2 cups

Enchiladas

Chicken Enchilada Casserole

1 chicken fryer
1 bay leaf
10 corn tortillas
Cooking oil
2 garlic cloves
1/8 teaspoon of cumin seeds
1 can cream of mushroom soup
1 can cream of chicken soup
1/2 cup tomato sauce
1/4 cup bell peppers
1/2 cup onions
1/4 cup tomatoes, chopped
2 serrano peppers, chopped
Salt
Pepper
2 cups sharp cheddar cheese, grated

Boil chicken with bay leaf and enough water to cover. De-bone and shred chicken. Reserve the water. Crush garlic cloves, cumin seeds and peppercorns. Heat skillet and add oil. Saute chicken with crushed spices, creamed soups, tomato sauce, bell peppers, onions, tomatoes and serrano peppers. Season to taste. Add some chicken stock and simmer. In another skillet, heat oil for the tortillas. Pass each tortilla on both sides do not leave in oil to fry. Set aside on paper toweling. Heat oven to 350 degrees. In a casserole dish, first line with corn tortillas then cover with chicken saute. Add a layer of creamed soups and then cheese. Repeat layers and top with cheese. Bake uncovered for 1 hour or until it is bubbling and cheese is melted.

Serves 8

Enchiladas With Beef And Cheese
Enchiladas de Res y Queso

Meat:
1 pound of stew meat, cubed
1 clove of garlic
1/4 teaspoon cumin seed
1/4 teaspoon black peppercorns
1/4 cup water
Salt
Pepper
3 tablespoons cooking oil
Corn tortillas

Crush garlic, cumin, and pepper corns to a smooth paste. Heat a skillet and add oil. Add meat and brown. Add spices, water and stir well. Cook for 25 minutes on medium heat. Simmer until juices are cooked off. Season to taste.

Sauce:
3 tablespoons chili powder
3 tablespoons flour
1 cup stewed tomatoes
3 tablespoons oil
2 cups water
3/4 teaspoon salt
Corn tortillas
3 cups Cheddar cheese, shredded

Heat oven to 350 degrees. Heat skillet and add oil. Stir in flour and brown. Stir in salt and chili powder. Remove from heat and add tomatoes and water. Place on heat and continue to simmer for 15 minutes. Heat another skillet and add oil. Pass each tortilla on both sides through oil and set aside. Do not fry. Fill each tortilla with beef and roll. Set these in a baking pan and pour sauce on them. Sprinkle more cheese and bake until cheese melts. Serve hot with beans and rice.

Serves 8

Enchilada Casserole

2 pounds lean ground beef
3 tablespoons chili powder
3 garlic cloves
1/4 teaspoon cumin seeds
1/4 teaspoon black peppercorns
3 tablespoons flour
1/4 small onion
1/2 small bell pepper
2 cups water
Salt
Corn tortillas
3 cups cheddar cheese, grated

Heat oven to 350 degrees. Crush or grind garlic, cumin and pepper corns. Heat a skillet and brown the ground beef. Then add onions, bell pepper, flour and ground spices. Stir well. Add chili powder and water and stir. Bring to a boil then simmer for ten minutes. Heat another skillet and add oil. Pass each tortilla on both sides through oil and set aside. Do not fry. In a baking dish, cover bottom with corn tortillas. Sprinkle cheese to cover then pour chili sauce. Repeat this until all ingredients are used. Sprinkle more cheese and bake for one hour or until bubbling and cheese is melted. Serve with flour tortilla chips and beans.

Serves 8

Enchiladas With Cheese
Enchiladas con Queso

3 tablespoons chili powder
3 tablespoons flour
1 cup stewed tomatoes
3 tablespoons oil
2 cups water
3/4 teaspoon salt
Corn tortillas
3 cups Cheddar cheese, shredded

Heat oven to 350 degrees. Heat skillet and add oil. Stir in flour and brown. Stir in salt and chili powder. Remove from heat and add tomatoes and water. Place on heat and continue to simmer for 15 minutes. Heat another skillet and add oil. Pass each tortilla on both sides through oil and set aside. Do not fry. Fill each tortilla with cheese and roll. Set these in a baking pan and pour sauce on them. Sprinkle more cheese and bake until cheese melts. Serve hot with beans and rice.

Serves 6

Enchiladas With Chili Meat
Enchiladas con Chili con Carne

2 pounds lean ground beef
3 tablespoons chili powder
3 garlic cloves
1/4 teaspoon cumin seeds
1/4 teaspoon black peppercorns
3 tablespoons flour
1/4 small onion, diced
1/2 small bell pepper, julienned
2 cups of water
Salt
Corn tortillas
3 cups cheddar cheese, grated

Heat oven to 350 degrees. Crush or grind garlic, cumin and peppercorns. Heat a skillet and brown the ground beef. Then add onions, bell pepper, flour and ground spices. Stir well. Add chili powder and water and stir. Bring to a boil then simmer for ten minutes. Heat another skillet and add oil. Pass each tortilla on both sides through oil and set aside. Do not fry. Fill each tortilla with cheese and roll. Set these in a baking pan and pour chili sauce on them. Sprinkle more cheese and bake until cheese melts.

Serves 8

Green Chicken Enchiladas
Enchiladas Verdes de Pollo

Sauce:
10 green tomatoes, *tomatillos*
2 jalapeno or serrano peppers
1 slice of bread
1 small banana
1/4 garlic clove
Coriander sprigs to taste
Salt

First peel the brown casing on the *tomatillos*. Simmer tomatoes and peppers in the same pot for ten minutes. In a blender, puree tomatoes, peppers, bread, banana, garlic and coriander. Season to taste.

Chicken Saute:
1 chicken fryer, sectioned
1 bay leaf
Corn tortillas
Cooking oil
2 garlic cloves
1/8 teaspoon cumin seeds
1/8 teaspoon peppercorns
1/4 cup onions
Salt
2 cups Monterrey Jack cheese, shredded
Sour Cream
Guacamole, see recipe

Heat oven to 350 degrees. Boil chicken with bay leaf. De-bone and shred chicken. Reserve the water. Crush garlic cloves, cumin seeds and peppercorns. Heat skillet and add oil. Saute chicken with spices. Season to taste. Add some chicken stock, then cook for a few minutes or until most of the juices are cooked off. Heat another skillet and add oil. Pass each tortilla on both sides through oil and set aside. Do not fry. Fill each tortilla with beef saute and roll. Set these in a baking pan and pour green sauce on them. Sprinkle cheese generously and bake until cheese melts. Serve with sour cream on top and complimented with guacamole.

Serves 6

The Mummies

One of the most unusual and certainly the most grisly place I've visited while traveling in Mexico was *La Calzada del Panteon*, or City Cemetery, located at the northwest end of the city of Guanajuato.

Anyone who has visited the area has probably been to see "The Mummies."

About one hundred years ago, Guanajuato ran out of room in its cemetery and the city decided to dig up those corpses whose families weren't around to pay to keep them in the ground.

The workers were shocked to find that the minerals in the earth had mummified the bodies.

The corpses were put on public display and a new tourist destination was born. Imagine, if you can, tourists paying to walk through room after room of dead people caught in horrorific poses and positions, with many of the visitors taking pictures with the dead, like you might take a photo with a movie star or famous athlete.

As you exit the exhibit, which I did relatively quickly, what is waiting outside is a bustling tourist industry where "mummy memorabilia" is offered for sale.

If you like gruesome and depressing, you'll give this place high marks, but it's not on my "hope to go back" list.

Miscellaneous

Bean And Cheese Open-faced
Sandwich
Empanadas Mexicanas

1 1/2 cup cooked pinto or black beans
Ground black pepper
Cooking oil
1 cup Monterrey Jack cheese, shredded
4 French bread slices

Heat skillet and add oil. On medium heat, add beans and stir occasionally for five minutes. Mash beans to a smooth consistency. Sprinkle with black pepper. If the mixture is runny add one teaspoon of flour at a time until the mixture is dry and smooth. Scoop out bread from center and fill with beans. Sprinkle with cheese and serve open faced for breakfast or as a snack.

Serves 2-4

Cactus In A Chili Sauce
Nopalitos con Chile

2 cups cactus, cleaned and diced
2 tablespoons onions, diced
2 tablespoons flour
1 tablespoon chili powder
2 garlic cloves
1/4 teaspoon cumin seeds
1/8 black peppercorns
3 tablespoons cooking oil
1/4 cup water
Salt
Pepper

Boil cactus for 15 minutes. Drain and rinse them thoroughly. Crush or grind garlic, cumin and peppercorns. Heat skillet and add oil. Saute onions and chili powder. Add flour and brown. Add water, spices and stir. Then add the cactus. Stir and cook for 5 minutes on low heat. Season to taste. Serve with warm corn tortillas.

Serves 4

Cactus And Egg
Nopalitos con Huevo

1 cup cactus, cleaned and diced
2 eggs
2 tablespoons onions, diced
1 hot pepper of choice, diced
2 tablespoons cooking oil
Salt
Pepper

Boil cactus for 15 minutes. Drain and rinse them thoroughly. Beat eggs in a bowl. Heat skillet and add oil. Saute onions, pepper and cactus for 3 minutes on low heat. Scramble eggs in with cactus and cook as desired. Season to taste. Serve with warm corn tortillas.

Serves 4

Cornbread
Pan de Maiz

1 cup cornmeal
1 cup flour
1 tablespoon sugar
2 teaspoons salt
1 tablespoon baking powder
2 eggs
1 cup milk
3 tablespoons oil
1/4 onion, diced
2 jalapeno peppers, chopped
3 slices bacon, sliced
1 cup sharp cheese, shredded
1 cup cream style corn

Heat oven to 375 degrees. Sift flour, sugar, salt and baking powder. Stir in cornmeal. Beat eggs and add milk and oil. Add this to dry ingredients. Heat a skillet and saute jalapenos, onions, and bacon. Combine all ingredients including cheese and corn and pour into baking dish. Bake for 40 minutes or until golden brown. Test a toothpick in the center of the cornbread until it is clean when removed.

Serves 6

Goat In Gravy
Cabrito Guisado

7-8 pound baby goat
Cooking oil
1 head of garlic
2 teaspoons cumin seeds
1 1/2 teaspoons black peppercorns
2 sweet onions, diced
3 tomatoes, diced
2 green bell peppers, diced
3 serrano or jalapeno peppers, chopped
1 tablespoons salt

A whole goat can be cut or sawed into pieces or it can be sent to a butcher shop to be cut. In any case, the bones need to be included in this recipe for the best flavor.

Crush or grind garlic, cumin and peppercorns. Heat a skillet and saute crushed spices, onions, tomatoes, bell peppers and hot peppers. In a large stew pot, brown the goat pieces. Then add saute mixture and stir. Add hot water to cover and cook on high heat. Bring to a boil and simmer until meat is tender. Add salt and stir well.

Gravy:
2 cups warm water
3/4 cup flour

In a large bowl add water and flour. Whisk or mix well until flour has dissolved. Pour this in the stew pot and stir. Heat thoroughly. Serve hot with rice, beans and tortillas.

Serves 10

Monterrey

Driving around in Monterrey is visually a lot like driving around a city in South Texas, where the billboards are displayed in both Spanish and English and most of the people are somewhat bilingual.

Monterrey is a city that is prospering in part from the location of U.S. manufacturing plants and north of the border businesses within its boundaries. Many of the things a visitor from yesteryear will recall still survive, such as the proliferation of street mimes, street actors, and street musicians.

One of the things that I think of when I remember Monterrey is eating *cabrito*, or goat. Local cooks are very proud of their preparation of this delicacy and most often the carcasses are baked over coals in the restaurant window facing the street.

Its an anglo prejudice that goat meat is less tasty than cow, pig, or chicken. *Cabrito*, like *Queso Flameado* made from goat's milk cheese, is a dish that should be tested before it is dismissed as too exotic for north of the border tastes.

Whenever traveling in or near Monterrey, try the *cabrito*, especially from the restaurants that cook the meat over open coals in plain sight. Don't be tempted by those who "barbecue" it so that the taste is hidden under a thick coating of sauce. *Cabrito*, like other meats, can be at its best when it is least adulterated.

Hot Dog Roll-Ups

6 frankfurters
6 corn tortillas
6 toothpicks
Cooking oil

Wrap a tortilla around each frankfurter and secure with a toothpick if needed. Heat skillet and add one cup of oil to fry. Once the oil is hot, fry each one until they are crispy on the outside. Place on a plate with paper towels. Remove toothpicks. Serve hot with chili with meat or mustard.

Serves 3-4

Hot Pepper Oil 1

1/2 quart olive oil
4 jalapeno peppers, punctured

Heat oil thoroughly then add peppers. Pour in a clean wine bottle and cover tightly. Let sit for 1 week. Covered tightly and stored in a cool place, this oil will last indefinitely.

Hot Pepper Oil 2

1/2 quart soybean oil
3 Jap or *chile japones*, punctured

Heat oil thoroughly then add peppers. Pour in a clean wine bottle and cover tightly. Let sit for 1 week. Covered tightly and stored in a cool place, this oil will last indefinitely.

Hot Pepper Oil 3

1 quart grape seed oil
2 Habanero peppers, punctured

Heat oil thoroughly then add peppers. Pour in a clean wine bottle and cover tightly. Let sit for 1 week. Covered tightly and stored in a cool place, this oil will last indefinitely.

Lenten Bread 1
Capirotada

2 loaves white bread
2 1/2 cups raisins
3 cinnamon sticks
1 cup brown sugar
4 cups water
3 cups cheese, shredded

Toast all pieces of bread and set aside. In a large saucepan boil raisins, sugar and cinnamon sticks in 4 cups of water. This will make a raisin tea. In a baking pan start with a layer of toast, then cover with cheese. Pour a ladle of tea to cover and repeat bread and cheese layers again covering with raisin tea. Once all the layers are finished, cover and let stand for 30 minutes. Serve warm or cold.

Serves 10

Lenten Bread 2
Capirotada

2 loaves white bread
2 1/2 cups raisins
1 cup apple, peeled and diced
3 cinnamon sticks
1 cup brown sugar
4 cups water
3 cups cheese, shredded
1 cup pecans, chopped
1 cup bananas, sliced

Toast all pieces of bread and set aside. In a large saucepan boil raisins, apples, sugar and cinnamon sticks in 4 cups of water. This will make a raisin tea. In a baking pan start with a layer of toast, then cover with cheese, pecans and bananas. Pour a ladle of tea to cover and repeat layers covering with raisin tea. Once all the layers are finished, cover and let stand for 30 minutes. Serve warm or cold.

Serves 10

Mexican Pigs In A Blanket

6 frankfurters
Flour tortilla dough, see recipe
6 toothpicks
Cooking oil

Fold out each tortilla and wrap around each frankfurter and secure with a toothpick if needed. Heat skillet and add one cup of oil to fry. Once the oil is hot, fry each one until they are golden on the outside. Place on a plate with paper towels. Remove toothpicks. These can also be baked. Heat oven to 350 degrees and bake until golden brown. Serve hot with chili with meat or mustard.

Serves 3-4

Mexican Pizza
Pizza Mexicana

4 flour tortillas, see recipe
1 cup refried beans, see recipe
1 cup cooked ground beef
2 cups of lettuce, chopped
1 1/2 cups tomato, diced
1 1/2 cup sharp cheddar cheese, shredded
1 cup guacamole, see recipe
1 cup sour cream
Optional:
Picante sauce

Heat skillet and add oil. Fry one tortilla at a time. Fry until golden brown and crispy. Set aside on a plate with paper towels. On each tortilla spread with warm, not hot refried beans. Sprinkle with ground beef and all other ingredients. Add picante sauce to taste. Mexican pizzas can be made as small or as big as you like for parties or other occasions.

Serves 4

Mexico City Pizza

Some readers will think that Mexican pizza is a joke, but it isn't, and I'm not the only one who makes it.

Not long ago, I spent a week in Mexico City. At least that's where I was told the plane landed. I couldn't actually see anything through the red and gray haze of polluted air that is forever lodged above what is now the world's largest metropolitan area and my eyes were watering too badly to be able to read any signs. (At the time, there was actually some public debate as to whether giant fans could be built to suck the offending air out of the Valley and dump it over the mountains on someone else.)

At our first meal that night, the waiter informed us that he had lived in the U.S. for several years, but that he came back to Mexico because he had grown tired of the high crime rate and the corrupt U.S. government. The food was a little better than the conversation.

By the end of the week, I was craving American pizza in the worst way. That night, I told our taxi driver to take us to the nearest Pizza Hut, and that's where I discovered that pizza in Mexico City may be somewhat different than that found in South Texas, but it was just as satisfying.

Turkey Mole

6-8 Turkey legs
1 bay leaf
1 cup almonds
1/4 cup sesame seeds
1 bread slice, toasted
1/4 cup raisins
1 tablespoon semi-sweet chocolate
1/8 teaspoon ground cloves
1 teaspoon ground cinnamon
1/4 teaspoon anise seed
4 tablespoons chili powder
6 tablespoons oil
1 onion, chopped
2 garlic cloves, chopped
2 tablespoons flour
1 can stewed tomatoes
Salt

In a large soup pot, boil turkey with bay leaf. In a large dry skillet add almonds and sesame seeds and toast on medium heat. Remove from heat when browned and add to a blender. Blend on high until smooth. To this add toast, raisins and chocolate. Blend on high until smooth. Heat another skillet and add oil. Saute onion and garlic. Then add flour. Stir until flour browns. Then add tomatoes and simmer. Pour these ingredients in blender with 2 cups of turkey broth. Blend until smooth. Return mole sauce to skillet and heat thoroughly. If the sauce is too thick, thin it out by adding more turkey stock. To this add the turkey and simmer for 15 minutes.

Serves 6-8

NOTE: At the time Cortez arrived, the Aztec had only bothered to domesticate two animals for human consumption, the dog and the turkey, or *Uexolotl*. The bird may have been introduced to Europe by Turkish traders who had come in contact with the Spanish, which would explain why it came to be called a turkey.

Pasta

Macaroni Ole

1 cup elbow macaroni
2 tablespoons cooking oil
3/4 cup tomato sauce
1 garlic clove
1/4 teaspoon cumin seeds
1/8 black peppercorns
1 pound lean ground beef
1 cup cheddar cheese, grated

Crush or grind garlic, cumin and peppercorns.
Heat a large skillet and add oil. Brown shells and
add spices and tomato sauce. Add beef and stir.
Cover with water and simmer until beef is cooked.
Do not over cook macaroni. Sprinkle cheese with
each serving.

Serves 6

Mexican Shells With Cheese
Conchas Mexicanas con Queso

1 bag of large shells
1 cup milk
1 egg
1 1/2 cups sharp cheddar cheese, shredded
1/2 onion (whole)
1/3 cup cooking oil
Salt

In a large pan or pot heat oil and brown shells. Cover with tap water. Add onion. Cook shells to your desire. In a bowl beat egg and add milk. Take onion out then add milk and egg mixture. Mix well until the egg cooks. Then add cheese and mix lightly. Cover and serve warm. If serving cold, refrigerate and serve on a bed of lettuce as a salad.

Serves 6

Mexican Style Spaghetti

8 ounces spaghetti
Cooking oil
2 garlic cloves, crushed
2 tablespoons chopped onion
1/2 teaspoon Italian seasoning
4 poblano peppers
1 cup stewed tomatoes
7 ounces white cheese, shredded
1 cup heavy cream
Salt
Pepper

Cook spaghetti as desired and drain. Heat skillet and add oil. Saute garlic, onion, Italian seasoning and whole peppers. Add tomatoes, cheese, cream and simmer. Remove peppers and season to taste. Serve spaghetti on each plate and pour sauce over.

Serves 4

Shells And Meat
Conchas con Carne

1 pound of stew meat, cubed
2 cups pasta shells
1/4 cup tomato, diced
1/4 cup onion, diced
2 garlic cloves
1/4 teaspoon cumin seeds
1/8 teaspoon peppercorns
2 tablespoons oil
2 1/2 cups water
Salt

Crush or grind garlic, cumin, and peppercorns. Heat skillet and oil. Brown shells and add tomatoes, onions, spices and meat. Add water and simmer until shells are cooked as desired. Season to taste.

Elbow macaroni can be substituted instead of shells. Also, more water is necessary if using larger shells.

Serves 4

Vermicelli And Beef Tips
Fideo con Carne de Res

5 ounces dry vermicelli
1/2 pound stew meat or ground beef
1/4 cup of tomato sauce
2 garlic cloves
1/4 teaspoon black peppercorns
1/4 teaspoon cumin seeds
1/4 onion, chopped
1/4 bell pepper, chopped
3 cups of hot water or beef broth
Salt
2 tablespoons cooking oil

In a skillet, brown meat, add onions and bell
peppers, then saute. Crush or grind all spices. In
a separate skillet, heat oil and brown vermicelli.
Add crushed spices, hot water, tomato sauce and
the ingredients of the other pan. Boil 20-30
minutes or until meat and vermicelli are tender.
Season to taste. Serve with warm flour tortillas
and beans.

Serves 4

Vermicelli And Chicken
Fideo con Pollo

5 ounces dry vermicelli
1/2 chicken, sectioned
2 tablespoons cooking oil
1/4 cup of tomato sauce
2 garlic cloves
1/4 teaspoon black peppercorns
1/4 teaspoon cumin seeds
1/4 onion, chopped
1/4 bell pepper, chopped
3 cups of hot water
Salt

Crush or grind all spices. Heat skillet and add oil. Brown the vermicelli. Add hot water, chicken pieces, tomato sauce, and spices. Stir and add all other ingredients. Boil 20-30 minutes or until chicken and vermicelli are tender and cooked. Season to taste.

Serves 4

San Miguel de Allende

For me, the most charming of Mexico's colonial cities is San Miguel de Allende, which looks today much like it did when it was built in the 1500s--if you subtract the automobiles and electric power lines.

We stayed at the *Casa de Sierra Nevada*, one of the most charming hotels I ever seen, which was managed by a Swiss man named Markus Odermatt and his Mexican wife.

San Miguel de Allende is one of those places that travelers quite literally fall in love with. That's probably why there are so many American artists, writers, and retirees who call the town home at least for a large part of each year. It is also a place that draws together people who might totally miss each other in a different environment.

That's how we met Frank, a U.S. ex-patriot living in La Paz on the Baja, who was there for a month so he could learn Spanish and communicate with his new girl friend.

We also became friends with Jay Kimball and his daughter Gretchen, who were returning from the coast where they had spent a season selling hot air balloon rides. Jay's mother was one of the writers who was blacklisted during the McCarthy era and had moved to Mexico. He and Gretchen had visited her grave in nearby Guanajuato.

How wonderfully strange it was that one morning at daylight Frank from the Baja, Markus from Switzerland, and a party of South Texans would ride with Jay in a hot air balloon over San Miguel de Allende while Gretchen gave chase in a truck.

When we last saw Jay and Gretchen, they were planning a balloon ride over the world's third largest pyramid at Teotihuacan outside Mexico City.

Pork

Fried Pork Tips
Carnitas

2 pounds pork, cut of choice in small pieces
Cooking oil
1/2 whole onion
1 cup milk
1/2 orange peel
4 coriander stems with leaves
Salt
Pepper

Heat skillet and add oil. Add pork with whole onion and brown real well. Remove onions and add milk, whole coriander, and orange peel. Stir and simmer uncovered for 1 hour and 30 minutes, or until fried well. Season to taste. Remove peel and stems. Place the meat in a large bowl and put with a paper towel to remove excess oil. Serve with corn tortillas and a hot sauce.

Serves 6

Mexican Sausage
Chorizo

6 garlic cloves
2 teaspoon black peppercorns
1 1/2 teaspoon cumin seeds
5 pounds coarse ground pork butt
2 tablespoons salt
1 1/2 teaspoon cayenne pepper
1/2 teaspoon nutmeg
1/2 teaspoon ginger
3 teaspoon sugar
1 cup raisins
1 cup cool water

Crush or grind garlic, peppercorns and cumin. In a large bowl combine crushed spices and all other ingredients. Mix thoroughly and stuff into long hog casing. Sausage must be cooked, baked or fried.

Chihuahua

Many people may recall a visit to the home of Pancho Villa as their most vivid memory of Chihuahua, but that isn't mine. Our guide, Katherine, was a former beauty queen who stood close to six feet tall and had blue eyes and blond hair. Her parents were Mennonites and she insisted that we visit their nearby settlements.

The Mennonites first moved to Mexico from Canada in 1922 after purchasing three hundred thousand acres of land. Their holdings doubled with a later purchase from publisher William Randolph Hearst.

Much of the produce of the area and a great amount of the milk products, especially cheese, found in Mexican markets is grown and processed by the Mennonites. The Chihuahua community of Mennonites has over sixty thousand members.

It is difficult to explain the fascination in visiting a Mennonite school in Mexico where little blue-eyed children do their classwork in German. Only the adult males in the community use Spanish, and only then in order to carry on commerce.

The visit was like turning a page back to a century ago in the U.S. when there was no electricity and every family had to grow and preserve their own food. The pantries were full of canned vegetables in glass jars. Milk cans filled from the morning chores sat outside every gate waiting to be picked up. Every yard seemed to have an apple tree filled with fruit.

Our guide had arranged for us to have lunch with a Mennonite family and we were presented with some of the best sausage and cheese I've ever eaten.

Pork And Broccoli

2 pounds pork shoulder, cubed
2 tablespoons cooking oil
2 garlic cloves
1/4 teaspoon cumin seeds
1/8 teaspoon black peppercorns
3 cups frozen or fresh broccoli
2 tomatoes
1/2 onion, diced
1/8 teaspoon cayenne pepper

Boil tomatoes. Puree tomatoes and onions in blender. Crush or grind garlic, cumin and peppercorns to a smooth paste. Heat skillet and add oil. Brown pork cubes and add tomato puree, spices and cayenne pepper. Stir and simmer. Add broccoli and 1/4 cup of water. Simmer until broccoli is tender to taste. Cook as desired. Serve hot with warm flour tortillas.

Serves 4

Pork Chops
Puerco Adovado

8 pork loin chops
Salt
Pepper
2 tablespoons flour
2 eggs
3 cups bread crumbs
Cooking oil

Sprinkle salt and pepper on both sides of pork chops. Then dust both sides of pork chops with flour. In a shallow bowl, beat both eggs. On a plate, empty the bread crumbs. Dip the pork chops in the eggs and then the bread crumbs. Set aside for 20 minutes. Heat oil in a skillet and when it is hot, deep fry each pork chop about 5 minutes or until it is cooked through. Drain on paper towels. Serve with vegetables of choice.

Serves 4

Pork In A Chili Sauce

2 pounds pork, cubed
2 tablespoons cooking oil
2 tomatoes
2 garlic cloves
1/4 teaspoon cumin seeds
1/8 teaspoon black peppercorns
3 jalapeno peppers
1/2 cup onion, chopped

Boil tomatoes and peppers. In a blender add onions, tomatoes and peppers and puree. Crush or grind garlic, cumin and peppercorns. Heat skillet and add oil. Brown pork and drain. Add spices, and tomato puree. Add 1/4 cup water and let simmer. Served over white rice.

Serves 4

Pork Tips In Green Sauce
Puerco en Salsa Verde

2 pounds pork shoulder, cubed
1 cup onion, diced
1 garlic clove
1/4 teaspoon cumin seeds
1/8 teaspoon black peppercorns
10 green tomatoes, *tomatillos*
2 jalapeno or serrano peppers
Coriander sprigs to taste
1/4 cup shelled sunflower seeds
1 cup chicken broth
1/2 cup water
1 teaspoon lime juice
Salt

First peel the brown casing on the *tomatillos*. Simmer tomatoes and peppers in the same pot for ten minutes. Do not let tomatoes split open or they will lose their flavor. Crush or grind garlic, cumin and peppercorns. In a blender, puree spices, tomatoes, peppers, coriander, sunflower seeds, broth, water and lime juice. Season to taste. Heat a skillet and add oil. Brown pork tips. Pour green sauce and simmer on low heat until the pork is done. Do not over cook. Serve hot with tortillas.

Serves 4

Pork Tips In Gravy
Guisado de Puerco

1 1/2 pounds of pork shoulder, cubed
1 tomato, diced
1 onion, diced
1/2 bell pepper, julienned
3 tablespoons flour
2 garlic cloves
1/4 teaspoon cumin seeds
1/4 teaspoon black peppercorns
Salt
Pepper
3 tablespoons cooking oil

Crush or grind garlic cloves, cumin, and peppercorns to a smooth paste. Heat a skillet and add oil. Add meat and brown. Cook for 20 minutes on medium heat. Add tomatoes, onions and bell peppers. Add flour and spices and stir well. To this add one cup of water and let it simmer another five minutes or until meat is tender. Season to taste. Serve with flour tortillas, beans and rice.

Serves 4

Pork Tips In Red Chili Sauce
Asado de Puerco

1 1/2 pounds pork butt, cubed
3 tablespoons chili powder
2 garlic cloves
1/4 teaspoon cumin seeds
1/4 teaspoon black peppercorns
Salt
Pepper
3 tablespoons cooking oil

Crush or grind garlic cloves, cumin , and pepper corns to a smooth paste. Heat a skillet and add oil. Add meat and brown. Add chili powder and cook for 20 minutes on medium heat. Add spices and one cup of water and let it simmer another five minutes or until meat is tender. Season to taste. Serve with flour tortillas, beans and rice.

Serves 4

Pork Tips And Squash
Carne de Puerco con Calabazita

1 pound pork shoulder, cubed
3 medium squash, sliced
1 can whole kernel corn
1/4 cup onion, diced
1/4 cup tomatoes, diced
2 garlic cloves
1/4 teaspoon cumin seeds
1/4 teaspoon black peppercorns
Salt
Pepper

Crush or grind garlic, cumin and peppercorns. Heat skillet and add oil. Brown meat and add all other ingredients including spices. Add 1/4 cup of water, cover and simmer. Keep from stirring frequently or it will turn to mush. Season to taste.

Serves 4

Salads

Avocado And Shrimp Salad
Enslaved de Camarones y Aguacate

3 avocados, peeled and cubed
1 cup cooked shrimp
2 scallions, minced
2 tablespoons coriander leaves, chopped
2 lemons
1 tablespoon olive oil
1 clove garlic, chopped finely
1 head of lettuce of choice

In a large bowl, combine avocados, shrimp, scallions and coriander. In a small bowl squeeze lemons and add oil and garlic. Mix well. Pour this over the avocado mixture and toss. Separate lettuce leaves and serve avocado mixture on top. Compliment with crackers of choice.

Serves 4

Bean Salad
Ensalada de Frijol

2 cups ranch style beans, cooked and drained
2 cups tomatoes, diced
1/2 cup onions, diced
1/4 cup coriander leaves
2 serrano peppers, chopped
3 limes
1 cup avocado, peeled and diced

In a large bowl mix all ingredients, except avocado. Cover and chill for 3 hours or overnight. Before serving squeeze limes and mix in avocados. Serve with corn tortilla chips.

Serves 6

Chicken Salad
Ensalada de Pollo

4 garlic cloves
1/4 teaspoon cumin seeds
1/8 black peppercorns
1 teaspoon dried oregano
1/4 teaspoon ground cinnamon
1/2 cup fresh lemon juice
2 jalapeno peppers, chopped
2 tablespoons tomato paste
4 boneless and skinless chicken breasts
3 cups thinly sliced leafy greens
1 cup tomatoes, diced
2 tablespoons toasted sesame seeds

Crush or grind garlic, cumin seeds and peppercorns. In a shallow dish combine lemon juice, peppers, tomato paste, oregano, cinnamon and crushed spices. Place chicken breasts in marinate and cover. Turn occasionally while refrigerating for one hour. Remove chicken and reserve marinate. Grill or broil chicken breasts as desired. In a skillet add marinate and bring to a boil. Cook for 1 minute. Cut chicken breasts in strips. In a bowl, toss greens and tomatoes. Serve chicken strips on top and sprinkle with sesame seeds. Compliment with corn tortilla chips.

Serves 4

Corn Chip Salad
Ensalada

4 cups lettuce, torn
4 cups small corn chips
1 can red beans, drained and rinsed
1 cup sharp cheddar cheese, shredded
1/4 cup french dressing

Optional:
Hot sauce

In a large salad bowl, toss all ingredients. Chill and serve as an appetizer. Add hot sauce if desired.

Serves 4

Crab Meat Garden Salad

6 ounces cooked or canned crab meat,
    drained and flaked
2 tablespoons olive oil
1 tomato, diced
1 onion, diced
1 serrano pepper, chopped
1/2 cup fresh coriander leaves
2 lemon

In a bowl mix crab meat, oil, tomato, onion, pepper and coriander. Squeeze lemon juice and stir. Natural juices are released and no water needs to be added. Serve chilled with corn tortilla chips.

Yields: 3 cups

Cucumber Salad
Ensalada de Pepinos

3 cucumbers
4 tablespoons sour cream
1 tablespoon vegetable oil
1 lemon
Salt
Lemon Pepper
Paprika

Peel and slice cucumbers. Rinse and chill. In a bowl mix sour cream, oil and lemon juice. Drain excess water and sprinkle with salt. Mix cucumbers in sour cream mixture and sprinkle with lemon pepper and salt. Serve chilled as an appetizer.

Serves 4

Fresh Green Salad
Ensalada Verde

4 cups lettuce, torn
1 can whole kernel corn, drained
1 can green peas, drained
2 avocados, peeled and cubed
2 tablespoons mayonnaise salad dressing
1 tablespoon lemon juice
1 large tomato, quartered

In a large salad bowl, mix all ingredients well, except tomatoes. Chill and serve. Each bowl should be topped with a tomato slice.

Serves 4

Fresh Summer Salad
Ensalada de Frutas

1/2 cup honey
1/3 cup fresh lime juice
3 cups watermelon, cut in balls
3 cups cantaloupe, cubed
3 cups honeydew melon, cubed
1 cup strawberries, halved
1 mango, peeled sliced

In a blender add honey and lime juice. Blend well. In a large, glass bowl toss fruit gently. Serve in wine glasses and drizzle honey mixture over the top.

Serves 10

Goat Cheese Salad
Ensalada de Queso de Cabra

4 ounces fresh goat cheese or farm cheese, cubed
1 cup tomatoes, diced
1/4 cup sweet onion, diced
Salt
Lettuce leaves
Crackers

In a bowl mix cheese, tomatoes and onion. Salt to taste. Chill and serve on a bed of lettuce. Compliment with crackers of choice.

Serves 2

Goat Cheese Sauce
Salsa de Queso de Cabra

4 ounces fresh goat cheese
2 tablespoons cooking oil
1 cup tomatoes, diced
1/4 cup sweet onion, diced
2 serrano peppers, chopped
1 garlic clove, chopped
Salt

Heat a skillet and add oil. Saute tomatoes, onions, peppers and garlic for three minutes. Crumble cheese into saute and stir. Simmer and cover. Do not over cook. Serve hot with warm corn tortillas.

Serves 2

Jicama Salad
Ensalada de Jicama

1 small jicama, peeled and cut into strips
1 orange, peeled and sectioned
1 cup watermelon, cubed
1 cup cucumbers, peeled and sliced
1 lemon
Salt
Cayenne pepper

Toss jicama, orange, watermelon and cucumbers. Then squeeze lemon juice and mix. Season to taste. Chill until ready to serve. Sprinkle lightly with cayenne pepper.

Serves 2

NOTE: The jicama root is brown and shaped like a beet. Within Mexico, it is often eaten raw with a dash of lime juice. The smaller ones are the sweetest and the larger they grow the more of a "woodish" texture they assume.

Papaya And Shrimp Salad
Ensalada de Papaya con Camarones

1/2 ripe papaya, seeded and cubed
3 ounces baby shrimp, peeled
1 tablespoon grated fresh coconut
1 lime
2 tablespoons coriander leaves, chopped
Cayenne pepper
Salt
Lettuce leaves

Place papaya on lettuce leaves and squeeze lime juice to cover. Then add shrimp and sprinkle coconut and coriander. Squeeze more lime juice. Season with cayenne and salt.

Serves 1

Pea Salad
Ensalada de Chicharos

1 can peas, drained
3 eggs
1/2 cup tomatoes, chopped
1/4 cup onions, chopped
1/2 cup mayonnaise
3 slices fried bacon, chopped

Boil eggs. Set aside and peel. Chop eggs and add in a bowl with peas, tomatoes, onions and mayonnaise. Blend well and chill. Serve on a bed of lettuce and sprinkle with bacon.

Serves 3

Potato Salad
Ensalada de Papas

4 potatoes
3 eggs
2 tablespoons dill relish
1/4 cup celery, diced
1/2 cup mayonnaise
1 1/2 tablespoon of mustard
Salt
Pepper

Optional:
1/4 pimento, chopped finely

In a large pot boil potatoes (whole, with skins) and add eggs. Boil until potatoes are tender. In a colander, drain run under cool water. Do not peel or dice potatoes until thoroughly cooled or they will turn to mush. Peel and dice potatoes. Peel eggs and dice. In a large bowl add all ingredients. If desired, add pimento. Toss well. Season to taste. Serve with steak or fajitas, rice and beans.

Serves 4

Shrimp Salad

1 pound shrimp, peeled and deveined
1 cup water
1/4 cup mayonnaise*
1/2 cup plain yogurt*
1 tablespoon lemon juice
3/4 cup cucumbers, sliced thin
1 scallion, sliced
Salt
Pepper
2 cups romaine lettuce, torn

In a saucepan bring water to boil. Remove from heat add shrimp. Poach for 4 minutes. Drain and chill for 1 hour. In a large bowl, combine mayonnaise, yogurt, lemon juice, cucumbers and scallions. *Use low fat if desired. Cut chilled shrimp in chunks and fold into mixture. Season to taste. Serve on a bed of lettuce.

Serves 4

South Texas Beef Skirt Salad
Enasalda de Fajitas de Res

Tortilla dough of choice
3-4 pounds of beef skirts*
1 can beer of choice
2 lemons
1/3 cup worcestershire sauce
Salt
Pepper
2 cups whole pinto beans, cooked and drained
Lettuce, shredded
Tomatoes, diced
Cheddar cheese, grated
Avocados, sliced
Optional:
Picante sauce

Some deep fryers come with a bowl-shaped shell maker. If yours does, then roll out tortillas and deep fry with the shell maker. Fry as many as needed and let them cool.

Take fat off the beef skirts. In a large bowl squeeze lemons, add beer, and worcestershire sauce. Let them marinate for one hour, but turn frequently. Season to taste. Grill or bake to your specifications. Slice fajitas against the grain in strips.

In each tortilla bowl, fill the bottom with beans, then layer with lettuce, tomato, cheese, fajitas and avocados. Add picante sauce if desired.

* Chicken breast may be substituted to make a chicken fajita salad.

Serves 4

Spinach And Cactus Salad
Ensalada de Espinacas y Nopalitos

1 cup cactus, cleaned and diced
2 cups raw spinach
3 eggs, boiled
1/2 cup fresh mushrooms, sliced
1/4 onion, diced
1/2 cup black olives, diced
2 teaspoons bacon bits
2 lemons

Boil cactus for 15 minutes. Drain and rinse well. Toss all ingredients together. Squeeze lemon juice and serve with crackers.

Serves 2

Tarahumara

The first Tarahumara Indian I ever talked with was pouring concrete on main street, the only one that's paved, in the village of Creel, which is located about a hundred miles or so southwest of Chihuahua (five hours by train).

He told me that he had worked in the construction business in Colorado, but that he had so many drunk driving citations that he couldn't go back to the U.S. without being arrested.

There were once many Indian tribes in the state of Chihuahua, including the Apache and the Conchos. When Chief Teporaca was defeated by the Spanish in 1653, many of the Tarahumara simply melted into the vast wilderness that is today called the Copper Canyon region of Mexico.

The canyon itself, which will one day be a major tourist attraction, is one and a half times deeper and spans four times the area of Arizona's Grand Canyon. Although it is now possible to drive there, most people arrive by rail. Within the protection of the canyons and its isolation live over fifty thousand Tarahumara Indians, who exist much as they have for centuries. American tourists can change that.

A tour of retirees from the southwest U.S. arrived at our hotel, *Posada Barrancas Mirador*, not long after we did. On their heels, three

Tarahumara gentlemen set up in the hotel lobby with a makeshift guitar strummer, a drum beater, and a "native" dancer, who shuffled around the room making grunting noises and later pretended to represent *El Toro*. The Americans hooted, applauded, and dropped coins in his hat.

The Tarahumara must think all Americans are rich fools.

Seafood

Breaded Fish
Milanesas de Pescado

6 fish fillets
2 cups bread crumbs
2 eggs
Oil
Salt
Pepper
Lemon wedges

In a large bowl beat eggs and season to taste. Put bread crumbs on a large plate. Pass each fillet in the egg mixture and then pat them into the bread crumbs. In a skillet heat oil and fry fish as desired. Serve with lemon wedges and a green salad.

Serves 6

Crab-Stuffed Avocados

1 cup crab meat
1/2 cup mayonnaise
1/2 cup celery, chopped
1 tablespoon onion, chopped
Pepper to taste
4 avocados
Lemon wedges

Mix all ingredients, except avocados and chill. Peel or leave avocado as is. If peeling, then serve on a bed of lettuce. Half the avocados and remove pit. Stuff avocados with crab mixture. Squeeze on lemon juice to taste. Chill until ready to serve.

Serves 8 as an appetizer

Fish Fillets In Garlic
Pescado al Mojo de Ajo

4 fish fillets, bass, snapper or perch
2 limes
Salt

In a shallow glass dish add fillets. Squeeze lime juice and sprinkle salt on the fish. Cover and refrigerate for 1 hour.

3 tablespoons unsalted butter
3 tablespoons olive oil
8 garlic cloves
1/2 cup flour
Salt
1 lime
2 tablespoons coriander leaves, chopped

Crush or grind garlic. Heat a skillet and add oil. Add butter and stir until it melts. Add garlic and saute, do not let it burn. Spread flour on a plate and salt to taste. Dredge the fillets and lay in the pan. Cook about 3 minutes on each side. Remove from heat and squeeze the lime juice on the fillets and sprinkle coriander. Return to heat for 1 more minute. Serve with white rice.

Serves 4

Flounder In Pepper Sauce

4 red bell peppers, sliced
1 tablespoon olive oil
1 cup water
4 cloves garlic, chopped
1/2 teaspoon dried basil
1/3 cup white-wine vinegar
2 green bell peppers, julienned
1 pound flounder fillets

Heat a skillet and add oil, red peppers, water, garlic, and basil. Cover and cook on medium heat until tender. Add this mixture and vinegar in a blender and puree. Heat oven to 450 degrees. Coat a baking dish with non-stick spray and add the fillets. Top fillets with green peppers and pour sauce to cover. Bake for 15 minutes or until the fish flakes easily with a fork. Serve with white rice.

Serves 4

Carmen Beach

One of my favorite rest stops on the Yucatan is *Playa del Carmen* (Carmen Beach), where one can order up a plate of fresh fish or shrimp and a cold bottle of *Dos Equis XX* while watching the ferry boats load and unload as they make their way to and from the island of Cozumel.

Virtually all visitors to the Cancun area will eventually go through the ferry port, which is also the port of choice by locals who work on the island. As a result, you'll see a curious mixture of tourists, Mexican laborers, and backpackers.

Among the backpackers, this beach isn't a side trip at all, but a destination within itself. The last time I was there, we met a retired Canadian who had opened a hammock hotel a few feet from the high water mark. For a couple of dollars a night, backpackers could rent a hammock and hang it between two of his poles. He also supplied lockers for gear and communal showers. He claimed to be making more money than he could spend.

One of the curiosities about *Playa del Carmen* is that it is a topless beach, which is somewhat rare in Mexico. Further north by about mile or so, we were told is a nude beach, but we did not investigate that claim.

When we asked the Canadian about his topless clientele, he said, "Oh, they're the Europeans. The ones who still have their clothes on are the Americans."

Regardless, the seafood at both *Playa del Carmen* and on the island of Cozumel is excellent.

Lemon Pepper Shrimp

1 tablespoon olive oil
1 tablespoon butter
1 garlic clove, crushed
1 lemon, quartered
1/4 teaspoon cayenne pepper
1 1/4 pound shrimp, peeled, de-veined and tail intact

Heat a skillet and add oil. Then add butter and stir until it is melted and hot. Add garlic and saute, do not let it brown. Remove and discard garlic. Squeeze lemon into pan and add wedges and cayenne pepper. Saute for 3 minutes. Remove lemon wedges and add shrimp. Saute until they curl and turn pink. Serve immediately.

Serves 4

Raw Fish
Ceviche

1 1/2 pounds red snapper
3 limes
2 garlic cloves
1/8 teaspoon black peppercorns
1/2 cup olive oil
1/2 teaspoon oregano
1/4 cup coriander leaves, chopped
2 serrano peppers, chopped
1 green bell pepper, julienned
2 tomatoes, diced
3 green onions, chopped

Cut fish into thin, small pieces. In a bowl, squeeze limes and marinate fish for 3 hours. Crush or grind garlic and peppercorns. In another bowl mix crushed spices, olive oil oregano, coriander and peppers. After the fish has marinated add this mixture. Then add onions and tomatoes. Stir gently and refrigerate for another hour. Serve on a bed of lettuce and top with avocados sliced thin.

*Fish can be marinated overnight.

Serves 4

Salmon-Ka-Bob

Fresh salmon, cut into two inch squares
Pearl onions, parboiled
Chunks green peppers, parboiled
Fresh mushrooms, lightly oiled
Lemons
Salt
White rice, see recipe

On long skewers, thread the fish and veggies in order of ingredients. Slide the skewers under the broiler. Broil or barbecue and turn frequently. Fish should flake easily when done. Squeeze lemon juice on salmon and salt to taste. Serve with white rice.

Serves 4

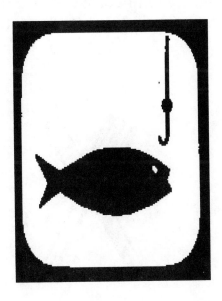

Salmon Patties
Albondigas

7 ounces pink salmon, drained
2 eggs
1/4 cup onion, finely chopped
2 tablespoons flour
Salt
Pepper
Cooking oil

Separate eggs. In a bowl mix egg whites until stiff. Beat egg yolks separately. In a separate bowl mix all ingredients including egg whites and yolks. Season to taste. Heat skillet and add oil. Form patties or scoop out a tablespoon of salmon mixture and fry until golden brown on both sides. Serve with french fries or baked potato and a fresh salad.

Serves 4

Sauteed Flounder

1 1/2 pounds flounder fillets
Olive oil
1 garlic clove, crushed
1/4 teaspoon cumin seeds
1/8 teaspoon black peppercorns
1 tablespoon lime juice
2 tablespoons coriander leaves, chopped
1 serrano pepper, chopped
1/4 teaspoon paprika
1 cup cooked salsa, see recipe
2 tablespoons sour cream

Crush or grind garlic, cumin and peppercorns. Heat a non-stick pan with 2 teaspoons of olive oil. Add fillets and saute for 3 minutes on each side. Remove fish from skillet and keep warm. Heat a small saucepan and add 1 tablespoon of oil. Then add crushed spices, lime juice, coriander, peppers, and paprika. Saute for 3 minutes and gently place fish in this pan. Spoon sauce mixture to cover. Heat thoroughly, but do not overcook. Serve with hot sauce and sour cream.

Serves 4

Shrimp And Bell Peppers
Camarones con Rajas

1 pound shrimp
1 onion, julienned
2 garlic cloves, chopped
2 tomatoes, diced
1/2 green bell pepper, julienned
Cooking oil
Salt
Pepper

Boil shrimp as desired and shell. Heat skillet and add oil. Saute onion and garlic, but do not let it brown. Add tomatoes and bell peppers. Season to taste. Add shrimp and cook for ten minutes. Serve with white rice

Serves 2-4

Shrimp With Flakes

2 pounds shrimp, shelled, de-veined, tails intact
1/4 cup lime juice
2 tablespoons crushed pepper flakes
1/4 cup olive oil
1/4 cup unsalted butter
4 garlic cloves, crushed

Optional:
1/2 cup Parmesan cheese, grated

In a bowl mix lime juice and pepper flakes. Heat a large heavy skillet and add oil. Then add butter. Stir until it is melted and hot. Add garlic and continue stirring, do not let garlic brown. Add shrimp and pour half of the lemon juice and pepper flakes on top. Cook shrimp for about 3 minutes and then turn them over and pour the mixture on the other side. When the shrimp are pink and start to curl. Remove from heat. Stir one last time and serve hot. Sprinkle with cheese if desired.

Serves 4

Veracruz

The first colonial city of Mexico was named *Villa Rica de la Vera Cruz*, or "Rich Town of the True Cross," by Hernan Cortes when he landed there in 1519. At the time, the area that is now the state of Veracruz was a province of the Aztec empire.

After making allies of the Totonac and other indigenous peoples, Cortes burned his eleven ships to symbolize to his 550 men that there was no turning back and proceeded to march inland to confront the Aztec.

One of Cortes' men was infected with the smallpox virus. This disease, which the indigenous people had no immunity from, would prove to be far more devastating than the Spanish sword. Millions of people died.

In this early period of colonialism, the Spanish began to supplement the labor force with Africans. By the time Jamestown was founded in the U.S., as many as 150,000 Africans or their descendants had arrived at the port of Veracruz. The influences of the Africans are not only seen in the *creole* look of many Veracruz residents, but in the African-Caribbean sounds of their music and their native dances, such as the *bamba, macumba, huapango,* and *cumbia.*

Veracruz has been compared to the U.S. city of New Orleans because a visitor can see the influence of the Spanish, French, African, and native people all coming together. Like New Orleans, Veracruz has the reputation of being a party town and the open air cafes in the downtown district are famous for their food, drinks, and hospitality.

The most memorable cuisine of this coastal city are seafood dishes such as *pescado huachinango a la veracruzano* (Veracruz Fish), *sopa de mariscos* (Seafood Soup), or *sopa de pescado* (Fish Soup).

Shrimp In Garlic
Camarones al Ajo

1 1/2 pounds shrimp
3/4 olive oil
3 garlic cloves
1/8 teaspoon black peppercorns
1 tablespoon minced parsley
1/2 teaspoon salt

Crush or grind garlic and peppercorns. Peel the shrimp, leaving the tail intact and de-vein. In a bowl add shrimp, oil, parsley, salt and crushed spices. Marinate for 1 hour. Heat a skillet and add mixture. Cook on high heat until shrimp are pink and curled. Remove from heat. Serve with white rice.

Serves 4

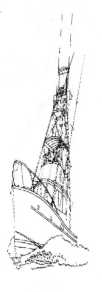

Shrimp Veracruz-Style
Camarones a la Veracruzana

Shrimp Marinate:
1 pound shrimp, peeled and de-veined
1/4 cup lime juice
1 garlic clove, crushed

Combine these ingredients in a large bowl. Cover and refrigerate for 1 hour. Stir occasionally.

Sauce:
1 tablespoon olive oil
1 garlic clove, crushed
1 cup onion, sliced in rings
1 bay leaf
1/4 teaspoon dried leaf thyme
1 teaspoon dried leaf oregano
1/2 cup pimiento stuffed olives
3 tomatoes, diced
1 cup semi-dry white wine
Salt

Heat skillet and add olive oil. Saute all ingredients for three minutes, except for wine. Add wine and simmer for 10 minutes or until thick. Add shrimp. Cover and cook until shrimp are pink and curled or about five minutes. Remove from heat. Serve with white rice.

Serves 4

Stir Fried Scallops

1 tablespoon peanut oil
1/2 cup red bell pepper, julienned
1/2 cup yellow bell pepper, julienned
1 cup green bell pepper, julienned
1 jalapeno pepper, julienned
1 cup onions, sliced thin
1 pound sea scallops
1 lemon
1 teaspoon olive oil
1 tablespoon soy sauce

Heat a skillet and add peanut oil. Stir-fry all peppers and onions for about 5 minutes. Remove vegetables and set aside. To the pan add the scallops and fry for 3 minutes. Squeeze lemon juice over the scallops. Add the vegetables to the skillet and add olive oil and soy sauce. Stir and cover for 2 minutes. Remove from heat. Serve hot with white rice (see recipe).

Serves 4

Soups

Chicken And Chickpea Soup

1 chicken fryer, sectioned
1 bay leaf
1 onion, quartered
1 carrot, sliced
2 teaspoons salt
1/8 teaspoon peppercorns, crushed
1 serrano pepper, whole
1 onion, cut in rings
2 green bell peppers, julienned
1 can chickpeas, drained
8 ounces Monterrey Jack cheese, cubed
1 avocado, peeled and cubed

In a large sauce pan add chicken, bay leaf, onion quarters, carrot, salt, peppercorns and serrano pepper. Add water to cover. Boil for 2 hours, stirring occasionally and skimming off fat. When chicken is done, remove the bay leaf, onion and serrano pepper. Then add the onion rings and bell pepper. Simmer for 10 minutes then add the chick peas. Simmer for 5 more minutes. In each bowl sprinkle cubed cheese and avocado. Serve with hot corn tortillas.

Serves 6

Chicken Noodle Soup
Caldo de Pollo

1 whole chicken, sectioned
1 bay leaf
2 whole stalks celery, sliced
2 carrots, peeled and sliced
1 whole onion
Coriander sprigs
1 1/2 cups egg noodles
Corn tortilla strips, see recipe
2 lemons
Salt
Pepper

In a large soup pot, add chicken pieces, bay leaf, celery, carrots, onion, and coriander sprigs. Bring this to a rolling boil then add noodles. Cook until noodles are tender, Season to taste. Serve each bowl with tortilla strips and a squeeze of lemon.

Serves 6

Chicken And Vegetable Soup
Sopa de Pollo y Vegetales

1 chicken fryer, sectioned
1/2 cup onion, diced
1/4 cup tomato, diced
1 garlic clove
1/2 bell pepper, julienned
1 potato, diced
2 carrots, sliced
Celery, diced
1/4 cup coriander leaves, chopped
1 1/2 cup mixed vegetables, drained
Salt
Pepper

In a blender add onion, tomato and garlic clove. Puree. In a large pot add chicken, puree and all other ingredients, except mixed vegetables. Add water to cover. Cook until vegetables and chicken are tender. Add mixed vegetables. Season to taste. Serve with corn tortillas.

Serves 4

Chickpea Soup
Sopa de Garbanzos

2 cans chickpeas, rinsed and drained
1 tablespoon vegetable oil
4 cups vegetable broth
2 garlic cloves
1/8 teaspoon black peppercorns
1/4 cup coriander leaves, chopped
1 cup onion, diced
1 cup milk
1 lemon
Salt
Pepper

Crush or grind garlic and peppercorns. In a heavy sauce pan heat oil and saute spices and onions. To the pot add chickpeas, broth, milk and coriander. Uncovered, bring pot ingredients to a simmer. Then cover and simmer for 20 minutes over low heat. Remove from heat and add to a blender. Blend until smooth. Return to heat and add lemon juice, salt and pepper to taste. If it is too thick add more milk or water. Serve with crackers.

Serves 4

Chili With Meat
Chili con Carne

2 pounds lean ground beef
3 tablespoons chili powder
3 garlic cloves
1/4 teaspoon cumin seeds
1/4 teaspoon of black peppercorns
3 tablespoons flour
1/4 small onion, diced
1/2 small bell pepper, julienned
2 cups of water
Salt

Crush or grind garlic, cumin and peppercorns. Heat a skillet and brown the ground beef. Then add onions, bell pepper, flour and ground spices. Stir well. Add chili powder and water and stir. Bring to a boil then simmer for ten minutes.

This chili is used best to top enchiladas, hot dogs, corn chips, burritos or fries.

Yields: 4-6 cups

Chili With Meat 2
Chile con Carne

2 pounds beef chuck, cubed
3 tablespoons chili powder
3 garlic cloves
1/4 teaspoon cumin seeds
1/4 teaspoon black peppercorns
3 tablespoons flour
1/2 teaspoon dried oregano
2 teaspoons paprika
1/2 small onion
1/2 small bell pepper
2 cups of water
1 cup tomato sauce
Salt
3 cups cheddar cheese, grated

Crush or grind garlic, cumin and peppercorns. Heat a skillet and brown the beef. Then add onions, bell pepper, flour and ground spices. Saute and stir well. Add chili powder, oregano, paprika, tomato sauce and water. Stir and bring to a boil then simmer for an hour. Sprinkle each bowl with cheese and serve with crackers.

*Beans may be added for chili beans.

Serves 6

Garlic Soup
Sopa de Ajo

2 heads of garlic, separated and peeled
6 cups chicken or vegetable broth
6 tablespoons vegetable oil
2 tablespoons olive oil
1/2 teaspoon thyme
1 bay leaf
1/8 teaspoon cayenne pepper
2 cups Parmesan cheese, grated
Salt
Pepper

Crush or grind garlic. In a heavy soup pot heat vegetable and olive oils. Add garlic, thyme and bay leaf. Simmer for 20 minutes. Pour out oil and reserve. To the soup pot add broth, salt and pepper to taste. Bring to a boil and strain. Return broth to pot and add cayenne pepper. Cover and serve hot. Sprinkle each bowl with Parmesan cheese. Serve with garlic or french bread.

Garlic bread may be made with the reserve oil by brushing sliced french bread with oil and baking it until golden brown.

Serves 4

Mexican Soup
Caldo

1 package of soup bones or oxtails
1 pound of stew meat
2 potatoes, cubed
3 carrots, cubed
1 cabbage, cut in quarters
4 corn on the cobs
1 tomato, cubed
4 celery stems, cubed
1 onion, diced
1 green bell pepper, julienned
Coriander sprigs to taste
Salt
Pepper
Optional:
2 zucchinis, diced
Lemons, sliced
Corn tortillas

In a large pot, boil soup bones and stew meat for 30 minutes. Add all the ingredients and boil for another 30 minutes or until the vegetables and meat have softened and cooked thoroughly. Season to taste. Serve in large soup bowls with lemon slices and corn tortillas.

Serves 6

Onion Soup
Sopa de Cebolla

4 cups sweet onions, sliced
3 tablespoons butter
1 tablespoon, flour
1 cup Monterrey Jack cheese with jalapenos,
    grated
Salt
Pepper

Heat oven to 350 degrees. In a large pot melt butter and add onions. Simmer for 45 minutes and stir constantly. Stir in flour until it dissolves. Add 4 cups of water and cover partially. Cook for 30 minutes. In oven safe bowls, serve each one with soup and top each bowl generously with cheese. Brown the cheese and serve with flour tortilla chips.

Serves 4

Potato Soup
Pure de Papa

4 potatoes, peeled and sliced
2 cups milk
1/2 cup water
2 tablespoons butter or margarine
1/4 cup onions, diced
1/4 cup celery, diced
1/4 cup American cheese, grated
Salt
Pepper

Boil potatoes until tender. Drain and add milk, water and butter. Simmer and add onions and celery. Stir until tender. Add cheese and stir until melted. Season to taste.

Serves 4

Tripe Soup
Menudo

2 beef or pork feet
5 pounds of tripe, cut in small squares
3 garlic cloves
1/2 teaspoon of cumin seeds
1/4 teaspoon black peppercorns
1 teaspoon oregano
3 tablespoons chili powder
1 large can of hominy
 1 1/2 tablespoons salt

Optional:
Onions, chopped
Lemons, sliced
Corn tortillas

Crush garlic, cumin seeds, and pepper corns, to a smooth paste. Remove any fat from the tripe and wash thoroughly. In a large pot, place the beef or pork feet in one gallon of water and boil for one hour. Skim fat as necessary. Add tripe and let it boil for another hour. Add spices and hominy and boil for another half hour. Serve hot and add any optional condiments.

Serves 4

Tripe Soup-Shortcut Menudo

2 beef or pork feet
5 pounds of tripe, cut in small squares
1 large can of hominy
4 tablespoons of menudo mix seasoning
Salt to taste
Optional:
Onions, chopped
Lemons, sliced
Corn tortillas

Remove any fat from the tripe and wash thoroughly. In a large pot, place the beef/pork feet in one gallon of water and boil for one hour. Skim fat as necessary. Add tripe and let it boil for another hour. Add all other ingredients and boil for another half hour. Serve hot and add any optional condiments.

Serves 4

Tortilla Soup
Sopa de Tortilla

4 corn tortillas, cut into strips
Cooking oil
2 garlic cloves, crushed
1/2 cup onion, diced
1/4 cup coriander leaves, chopped
2 cups chicken broth
1 1/2 cups tomato puree
Salt
Pepper
1/2 cup Monterrey Jack cheese, grated
1 avocado, peeled, seeded, and cubed

Heat 1/4 inch of oil and fry tortilla strips and set aside on paper towels. Heat a saucepan with oil and saute onion and garlic until softened. Stir in chicken broth and tomato puree and bring to a boil, then simmer for five minutes. Add coriander and season to taste. Serve by placing tortilla chips at the bottom of each bowl and pouring soup. Sprinkle cheese and top with avocado cubes.

Serves 4

Vermicelli Soup
Sopa de Fideo

2 pounds tomatoes
5 ounces dry vermicelli
2 garlic cloves
1/4 teaspoon cumin seeds
1/4 teaspoon black peppercorns
1 tablespoon olive oil
1 cup onion, diced
1/4 teaspoon thyme
1 tablespoon tomato paste

In a sauce pan boil tomatoes. Then add in blender and puree. Crush or grind garlic, cumin and peppercorns. In a skillet add oil and brown vermicelli. Add spices and onions. Stir well. Add thyme and tomato paste. Add all ingredients and simmer until vermicelli tender, but not mushy.

Serves 4

Vermicelli Soup
Sopa de Fideo

5 ounces dry vermicelli
2 garlic cloves
1/4 teaspoon black peppercorns
1/4 teaspoon cumin seed
1/4 onion, chopped
1/4 bell pepper, chopped
1 serrano pepper, chopped
3 cups hot water
4 cups chicken broth
1/4 cup tomato sauce
Salt
2 tablespoons cooking oil

Crush or grind all spices. In a pan brown the vermicelli with cooking oil, stir frequently not letting the vermicelli burn. Then add crushed spices, onions, bell peppers and serrano pepper. Saute, slowly adding the tomato sauce. Add hot water and chicken broth. Boil 20-30 minutes or until vermicelli is tender. Season to taste.

Serves 4

Cancun

Of all the wonderful destinations available, more Americans have seen Cancun than any other Mexican City. Almost two million of us go there each year, and the numbers are growing.

However, it is probably the least Mexican of all the cities in the country. It was built from scratch beginning in the late 1960s with American tourism in mind. Every U.S. fast food chain you can imagine has an outlet in Cancun. You will have to look for someone who <u>doesn't</u> speak English.

You won't find a central *zocalo*, a colonial era church, or anyone selling goat cheese from the roadside in Cancun. And don't worry about the conversion rate either. Your credit cards will be all you need to enjoy some of the world's best beaches and finest, though not inexpensive, dining.

Cancun, like Acapulco, is a party town. A week in Cancun is a daily *siesta* on the beach followed by a fine meal and a night on the town. You may get the feel that you are in Florida instead of a foreign country.

Most of the nearby diversions also cater to the American tourist rather than a student of Mexican culture.

One of the most enjoyable side trips I have taken while staying in Cancun was to the *Sian Ka'an* Biosphere Reserve, which lies on a huge limestone flat a few hours south of the city. The Biosphere represents a new way of thinking about Mexico's natural resources. Eco-tourism may become a reality for Mexico in years to come. I can tell you that the area of the Reserve that I was lucky enough to visit, with official sanction and a guide, was so pristine that you couldn't even find a gum wrapper and I made sure I left it that way.

Tamales

Tamales

Filling:
3 pounds chicken, chopped beef, or pork
5 pasilla peppers, seeded
4 garlic cloves
2 teaspoons cumin seeds
1 teaspoon black peppercorns
Salt to taste

Boil meat of choice and reserve liquid. In a meat grinder, grind meat. Boil peppers in a separate pot, then add in a blender and puree. Crush or grind garlic, cumin and peppercorns to a smooth paste. In a skillet without adding oil, brown meat and add pepper puree and spices. Stir frequently, simmer and cover.

Dough:
Corn shucks for wrapping
2 1/2 cups corn tortilla mix
2 teaspoons chili powder
1 cup shortening
1 1/4 cup reserve beef , chicken or pork broth
Salt to taste

Separate corn shucks, discard corn silk and soak shucks in hot water for 1/2 hour or until soft and pliable. Beat shortening until fluffy. Then add corn mix, chili powder, broth and salt to taste. Knead these ingredients until fluffy. If it is too dry add more broth.

To assemble, spread one tablespoon of dough on each shuck. Dough should be spread on the upper 3/4 of the shuck, leaving the pointed end without dough. Then spread a tablespoon of meat on one end. Then roll and fold over the end. Steam tamales in a colander. Do not let tamales get wet. Boil for an hour or until dough is cooked or tender, but not mushy.

Yield: 2 dozen tamales

Tamales

Filling:
2 cups raisins
5 apples, cubed
1 cinnamon stick

Boil all ingredients and reserve liquid.

Dough:
Corn shucks for wrapping
2 1/2 cups corn tortilla mix
2 teaspoons chili powder
1 cup shortening
1 1/4 cup reserve liquid
Sugar to taste

Separate corn shucks, discard corn silk and soak shucks in hot water for 1/2 hour or until soft and pliable. Beat shortening until fluffy. Then add corn mix, chili powder, reserve liquid and salt to taste. Knead these ingredients until fluffy. If it is too dry add more broth.

To assemble, spread one tablespoon of dough on each shuck. Dough should be spread on the upper 3/4 of the shuck, leaving the pointed end without dough. Then roll and fold over the end. Steam tamales with reserve liquid in a colander. Do not let tamales get wet. Boil for an hour or until dough is cooked or tender, but not mushy.

Yield: 2 dozen tamales

Tamales Blancos

Dough:
Corn shucks for wrapping
2 1/2 cups corn tortilla mix
2 teaspoons chili powder
1 cup shortening
1 1/4 cup reserve beef , chicken or pork broth
Salt to taste

Separate corn shucks, discard corn silk and soak shucks in hot water for 1/2 hour or until soft and pliable. Beat shortening until fluffy. Then add corn mix, chili powder, broth and salt to taste. Knead these ingredients until fluffy. If it is too dry add more broth.

To assemble, spread one tablespoon of dough on each shuck. Dough should be spread on the upper 3/4 of the shuck, leaving the pointed end without dough. Then roll and fold over the end. Steam tamales in a colander. Do not let tamales get wet. Boil for an hour or until dough is cooked or tender, but not mushy.

Yield: 2 dozen tamales

Tamales Borrachos

Filling:
3 pounds chicken, chopped beef, or pork
5 pasilla peppers, seeded
7 serrano or arbol peppers
4 garlic cloves
2 teaspoons cumin seeds
1 teaspoon black peppercorns
Salt to taste

Boil meat of choice and reserve liquid. In a meat grinder, grind meat. Boil peppers in a separate pot, then add in a blender and puree. Crush or grind garlic, cumin and peppercorns to a smooth paste. In a skillet, without adding oil, brown meat and add pepper puree and spices. Stir frequently, simmer and cover.

Dough:
Corn shucks for wrapping
2 1/2 cups corn tortilla mix
2 teaspoons chili powder
1 cup shortening
1 1/4 cup reserve beef, chicken or pork broth
Salt to taste

Separate corn shucks, discard corn silk and soak shucks in hot water for 1/2 hour or until soft and pliable. Beat shortening until fluffy. Then add corn mix, chili powder, broth and salt to taste. Knead these ingredients until fluffy. If it is too dry add more broth.

To assemble, spread one tablespoon of dough on each shuck. Dough should be spread on the upper 3/4 of the shuck, leaving the pointed end without dough. Then spread a tablespoon of meat on one end. Then roll and fold over the end. Steam tamales in a colander. Do not let tamales get wet. Boil for an hour or until dough is cooked or tender, but not mushy.

Yield: 2 dozen tamales

Real de Catorce

One of the most enchanting places that I have visited in Mexico is the near deserted mining town of Real de Catorce, which is located in the state of San Luis Potosi, near the town of Matehuala.

Less than a thousand people live there today, but it once was the home of 40,000 people, many of them wealthy Spaniards who built the town to European standards, complete with a Cathedral, stone streets, a bull ring, amphitheater, and even an opera house. There was a time when the city even minted its own money. The building which housed the mint still stands, but it was locked and boarded up when I was last there.

Getting to the city is a story within itself. From Matehuala, a desolate cobblestone road stretches over ten miles off the main highway into the high mountain desert before ascending to over 9,000 feet into the Sierra Madre Mountains. A narrow tunnel, one lane for automobiles, winds its way almost two miles through the mountain and leads to Real de Catorce.

Unlike San Miguel de Allende, this colonial city did not survive. It was virtually abandoned sometime after 1900. Local legend is that bandits controlled the town during that period.

About the only thing that has kept every building from collapsing and having goat herds rummaging in the ruins has been the thousands and thousands of Mexicans who make an annual pilgrimage each October on St. Francis of Assisi day to pay homage to the town's patron saint, whose statue in *La Parroquia de la Purisma Conception* is the town's best known resident.

There are only two small hotels in the city and the pilgrims leave camp out for days on the streets and in the ruins, leaving an incredible amount of human waste and trash, which the rains obligingly wash into the large gorge below the streets, where it will rest forever.

When I was last there, one gentleman who claimed to be an official told us that Real de Catorce would someday be rebuilt as a historical theme city, like Williamsburg, Virginia in the U.S. My guess is that it will take more than a few tour buses out of South Texas to make that happen.

Tortilla Dishes & Appetizers

Bean And Mexican Sausage Burritos
Burritos de Chorizo y Frijoles

Dough for flour tortillas (See recipe)
3 cups refried beans (See recipe)
3 links of Mexican sausage
2 cups cooking oil

Heat skillet and brown sausage thoroughly. Add beans in the same pan and stir occasionally for about five minutes. Mash beans and sausage until they are smooth. Roll out tortilla dough balls and fill each one with bean and sausage mixture. Close both ends inward, then roll tortillas. Heat oil in a separate skillet and fry the burritos until golden brown on both sides.

Serves 4

Bean And Mexican Sausage Burritos Deluxe
Burritos de Chorizo y Frijoles

Dough for flour tortillas, (See recipe)
3 cups refried beans, (See recipe)
3 links of Mexican sausage
2 cups cooking oil
2 cups chile with meat, (See recipe)
2 cups lettuce, shredded
2 cups tomato, diced
2 cups cheddar cheese, shredded

Heat skillet and brown sausage thoroughly. Add beans in the same pan and stir occasionally for about five minutes. Mash beans and sausage until they are smooth. Roll out tortilla dough balls and fill each one with bean and sausage mixture. Close both ends inward, then roll tortillas. Heat oil in a separate skillet and fry the burritos until golden brown on both sides. Top each with chile and cheese and lettuce and tomato.

Serves 8

Beef Roll-Ups
Flautas de Res

1 pound stew meat, cubed
1 garlic clove
1/4 teaspoon cumin seeds
1/4 teaspoon black peppercorns
1/4 cup water
Salt
Pepper
3 tablespoons cooking oil
Corn tortillas

Crush garlic, cumin, and peppercorns to a smooth paste. Heat a skillet and add oil. Add meat and brown. Add spices, water and stir well. Cook for 25 minutes on medium heat. Simmer until juices are cooked off. Season to taste. Let the meat cool and dry. Shred and fill each corn tortilla with meat and secure with a toothpick. Heat another skillet with oil and fry until golden brown on both sides. Serve with guacamole.

Serves 10

Chalupas

4 corn tortillas (See recipe)
1 cup refried beans (See recipe)
1 1/2 cups lettuce, chopped
1 cup tomato, diced
1 cup sharp cheddar cheese, shredded
Optional:
Picante sauce
Sour cream
1/2 cup guacamole (See recipe)

Heat skillet and add oil. Fry one tortilla at a time.
Fry them flat, until golden brown and crispy. Set
aside on a plate with paper towels. On each
tortilla spread with warm, not hot refried beans.
Sprinkle with all other ingredients. Add picante
sauce, sour cream, and guacamole.

Serves 2

Chalupas Deluxe
Chalupas Compuestas

4 corn tortillas (See recipe)
1 cup refried beans (See recipe)
1 cup cooked ground beef
2 cups lettuce, chopped
1 1/2 cups tomato, diced
1 1/2 cup cheddar cheese, shredded
1 cup guacamole (See recipe)
1 cup sour cream
Optional:
Picante sauce

Heat skillet and add oil. Fry one tortilla at a time.
Fry them flat, until golden brown and crispy. Set
aside on a plate with paper towels. On each
tortilla spread with warm, not hot refried beans.
Sprinkle with ground beef and all other
ingredients. Add picante sauce to taste.

Serves 2-4

Chicken Roll-ups
Flautas de Pollo

1 chicken fryer
1 bay leaf
Corn tortillas
Cooking oil
2 garlic cloves
1/8 teaspoon cumin seeds
1/4 cup onions, diced
Salt
Pepper

Optional: Sour Cream, Guacamole

Boil chicken with bay leaf. De-bone and shred
chicken. Reserve the water. Crush garlic cloves
and cumin seeds. Heat skillet and add oil. Saute
chicken with crushed spices. Season to taste . Add
some chicken stock, then cook for a few minutes
or until most of the juices are cooked off. Let
chicken cool and dry. Fill each tortilla with
chicken saute, roll and secure with a toothpick. In
another skillet, heat oil and fry on both sides or
until golden brown. Dip in sour cream or
guacamole.

Serves 4-5

Chilaquiles

12 corn tortillas
2 tablespoons of cooking oil
1/2 cup onion, diced
1 teaspoon sugar
3 ancho peppers, seeded and peeled
1 cup Mexican white cheese, crumbled
2 eggs, beaten
Salt
Pepper

In a bowl soak peppers in water. Cut tortillas in small squares. In a skillet, heat oil and fry tortillas. Add onions. Simmer and stir. In a blender add sugar, peppers with water and puree. Add puree to frying tortillas and stir. Stir in cheese and cover. Cook juices off and stir in eggs. Cook eggs to desired consistency. Serve hot with refried beans.

Serves 3

Corn Tortillas
Tortillas de Maiz

2 cups corn tortilla mix*
1 cup water

Add tortilla mix and water and knead well. If it is too sticky add more mix, if it falls apart add 1 teaspoon of water at a time until it holds together. Separate and form into balls. Using a clean, plastic grocery bag, cut a 10x12 inch piece of plastic. Place a dough ball between the plastic and use tortilla press. If you do not have a tortilla press, do not remove from plastic wrap. Roll out with rolling pin until thin. Coat griddle with non-stick spray and heat on high. Cook each corn tortilla until lightly browned but not hard or crispy.

*Corn tortilla mix or Masa Harina is a ready to use product that may be found in the specialty food section.

Yields: 12 corn tortillas

Corn Tortilla Chips
Totopos

12 corn tortillas, quartered
2 cups cooking oil
Optional:
Salt
Picante sauce

Heat skillet and add oil. Test the oil with one chip to make sure it is hot. Fry several pieces at a time and set aside on a plate with some paper towels. Add optional ingredients and serve with any meal.

Serves 6

Corn Tortilla Chips with Cheese Nachos

6-8 corn tortillas, quartered
2 cups cooking oil
8 ounces American cheese, cubed
1/4 cup milk
Optional:
Salt
Jalapenos, sliced

Heat skillet and add oil. Test the oil with one chip to make sure it is hot. Fry several pieces at a time and set aside on a plate with some paper towels. In a sauce pan warm milk on low heat and add cheese. Stir until the cheese melts and the sauce is smooth, add more milk if necessary. In each bowl add chips, pour cheese and jalapenos.

Serves 4-6

NOTE: Although making tortillas by hand is relatively simple, they will not always come out completely round unless you use a tortilla press, which is a small, inexpensive cast iron utensil that presses the ball of mix out evenly is all directions.

Corn Tortilla Chips With Beans And Cheese
Panchos

6-8 corn tortillas, quartered
2 cups cooking oil
1/2 cup refried beans, (See recipe)
8 ounces of American cheese, cubed
1/4 cup milk
1 cup guacamole, (See recipe)
Optional:
Salt
Jalapenos, sliced

Heat skillet and add oil. Test the oil with one chip to make sure it is hot. Fry several pieces at a time and set aside on a plate with some paper towels. In a sauce pan warm milk on low heat and add cheese. Stir until the cheese melts and the sauce is smooth, add more milk if necessary. Spread warm beans on each chip. If the beans are too hot the chips will become soggy. On a plate, add chips with beans, pour cheese and add jalapenos. Top off with guacamole and season to taste.

Serves 4-6

Deviled Eggs

6 Eggs
2 tablespoons dill relish
1 tablespoon mustard
2 tablespoons mayonnaise
Salt
Paprika

In a large pot, boil eggs. Drain and cool. Shell eggs and cut lengthwise. Remove yolks and place in a separate bowl. Crush or mash the yolks. To the yolks add the rest of the ingredients and mix well. Season to taste. Fill the hollow egg whites with mixture and sprinkle with paprika. Chill and serve as an appetizer.

Serves 4

Fast Flour Tortillas
Tortillas de Masa

2 cups flour tortilla mix*
1/2 cup warm water

In a large bowl add flour and warm water a little at a time until the dough starts to form. Knead well. Cover dough with plastic wrap or cloth. Allow to sit for 30 minutes. Separate dough into little balls, *testales*, and knead each one. Before rolling dough, make sure to flour the rolling pin and board. Roll out each ball as thin as possible. Turn griddle(s) on medium to high heat. Cook each tortilla on both sides until brown spots have formed. Stack and cover. Compliment with any meal or eat as a snack.

*Flour tortilla mix is a ready to use product that contains flour, baking powder and salt.

Yields:10-12 tortillas

Fiesta Cheese Ball

16 ounces softened cream cheese
2 cups sharp cheddar cheese, grated
1 tablespoon pimento, chopped
1 tablespoon green pepper, chopped
1 tablespoon onion, chopped
2 tablespoon worcestershire sauce
1 tablespoon lemon juice
1/8 teaspoon cayenne pepper
1/8 teaspoon salt
1/8 teaspoon garlic salt
1/2 cup pecans, finely chopped

In a large bowl mix cheeses well. Stir in remaining ingredients except pecans. Chill in refrigerator. Shape into ball and roll in pecans. Serve with corn or flour tortilla chips or fresh vegetables.

Serves 12

Flaming Cheese With Sausage Bits
Queso Flameado con Chorizo

8 ounces white cheese of choice, cubed
1/2 link of Mexican sausage
Flour or Corn Tortillas

Heat a skillet, brown sausage and cook well. Drain oil from sausage. Place cheese cubes in a microwave-safe dish. Heat on high setting until cheese melts. Add sausage in the middle of the dish and serve sizzling hot with tortillas.

Serves 2

Flour Tortillas
Tortillas de Masa

2 cups flour
1/3 cup shortening
1/4 teaspoon salt
1 1/2 tablespoons baking powder
1/2 cup hot water

In a large bowl add flour, salt and baking powder. Mix well with hands or whisk. Add shortening and knead thoroughly. Add warm water a little at a time until the dough starts to form. Knead well. Cover dough with plastic wrap or cloth. Allow to sit for 30 minutes. Separate dough into little balls, *testales*, and knead each one. Before rolling dough, make sure to flour the rolling pin and board. Roll out each ball as thin as possible. Turn griddle(s) on medium to high heat. Cook each tortilla on both sides until brown spots have formed. Stack and cover. Compliment with any meal or eat as a snack.

Yields: 10-12 tortillas

Flour Tortilla Chips
Tostadas

12 flour tortillas, quartered
2 cups cooking oil
Optional:
Picante sauce
Cheddar cheese, grated

Heat skillet and add oil. Test the oil with one chip and fry up to 5 tortilla pieces at a time. Fry until golden brown and set aside on a plate with some paper towels. Serve with optional ingredients.

Serves 6

Flour Tortilla Fritters
Bunuelos

2 cups flour
1/3 cup shortening
1/4 teaspoon salt
1 teaspoons baking powder
1/2 cup hot water
1/4 cup sugar
1 tablespoon cinnamon
Cooking oil

In a large bowl add flour, salt and baking powder. Mix well with hands or whisk. Add shortening and knead thoroughly. Add warm water a little at a time until the dough starts to form. Knead well. Cover dough with plastic wrap or cloth. Allow to sit for 30 minutes. Separate dough into little balls, *testales*, and knead each one. Before rolling dough, make sure to flour the rolling pin and board. Roll out each ball as thin as possible. In a skillet heat oil 1/4 inch thick. Leave whole or cut tortillas in strips, triangles or use cookie cutters. Fry tortilla pieces on both sides until golden brown. On a plate mix sugar and cinnamon together. Sprinkle this mixture on tortilla fritters. Store them in an air tight container to keep them from getting soggy.

Yields:10-12 whole tortilla fritters

Gorditas With Beans Panuchos

6 gorditas (See recipe)
1 1/2 cup cooked pinto or black beans
Ground black pepper
Cooking oil
Optional for stuffing:
Shredded beef or chicken
Cheese of choice

Heat oven to 350 degrees. Heat skillet and add oil. On medium heat, add beans and stir occasionally for five minutes. Mash beans to a smooth consistency. Sprinkle with black pepper. If the mixture is runny add one teaspoon of flour at a time until the mixture is dry and smooth. Slit the side of each gordita and stuff with refried beans or stuffing of choice. Place stuffed gorditas on a baking sheet and bake for 15 minutes or until thoroughly heated. Serve for breakfast with eggs and hot sauce.

Serves 6

Gorditas With Chicken
Gorditas con Carne de Pollo

6 gorditas (See recipe)
Chicken Saute:
1 chicken fryer, sectioned
1 bay leaf
Corn tortillas
Cooking oil
2 garlic cloves
1/8 teaspoon cumin seeds
1/8 teaspoon peppercorns
1/4 cup onions
Salt

Optional:
Green sauce (See recipe)
Monterrey Jack cheese, shredded

Heat oven to 350 degrees. Boil chicken with bay leaf. De-bone and shred chicken. Reserve the water. Crush garlic cloves, cumin seeds and peppercorns. Heat skillet and add oil. Saute chicken with spices. Season to taste. Add some chicken stock, then cook for a few minutes or until most of the juices are cooked off. Make a slit lengthwise and fill each gordita with chicken saute. Place stuffed gorditas on a baking sheet and bake for 15 minutes or until thoroughly heated. Pour green sauce on them and sprinkle cheese.

Serves 6

Homemade Corn Tortilla Chips
Totopos de Tortillas de Maiz

2 cups corn tortilla mix*
1 cup water
Cooking oil
Salt

Add tortilla mix and water and knead well. If it is too sticky add more mix, if it falls apart add 1 teaspoon of water at a time until it holds together. Separate and form into balls. Using a clean, plastic grocery bag, cut a 10x12 inch piece of plastic. Place a dough ball between the plastic and use tortilla press. If you do not have a tortilla press, do not remove from plastic wrap. Roll out with rolling pin until thin. Coat griddle with non-stick spray and heat on high. Cook each corn tortilla until lightly browned but not hard or crispy. Cut tortillas in triangles or strips. In a skillet heat oil and deep fry tortilla wedges until golden and crispy. Set aside on a plate with paper towels. Salt to taste and serve with a hot sauce.

*Corn tortilla mix is a ready to use product that may be found in the specialty food section.

Serves 6

Home-Style Quesadillas
Quesadillas

2 cups flour tortilla mix
2 tablespoons all purpose flour
1/2 teaspoon baking powder
Salt to taste
1/2 teaspoon butter, melted
1 egg
1/2 cup milk
8 ounces cheese of choice

In a large bowl add flour mix, flour, baking powder and salt. Mix thoroughly. Add butter, egg and enough milk to knead the dough firmly. Heat griddle on medium heat. Form dough balls and roll out into tortillas. Fill each tortilla with cheese and fold in half. Toast each tortilla on the griddle to a golden brown.

Yields 8 quesadillas

Plump Corn Tortillas
Gorditas

2 cups corn tortilla mix
1 1/4 hot water
1/2 cup shortening
Optional:
Salt
Butter or margarine

In a large bowl add corn tortilla mix and stir in water a little at a time while kneading dough into a ball. Knead shortening until dough ball is smooth. Make medium size balls and pat out into small, thick pancakes. Spray griddle with non-stick spray and heat on high. Cook each tortilla until golden on both sides. Lightly butter and salt. Serve warm as a bread.

Yields: 6 gorditas

Pork Roll-Ups
Flautas de Puerco

1 pound of pork butt, cubed
1 garlic clove
1/4 teaspoon cumin seeds
1/8 teaspoon black peppercorns
Salt
Pepper
3 tablespoons cooking oil
Corn tortillas

Crush garlic, cumin and peppercorns to a smooth paste. Heat a skillet and add oil. Add meat and brown. Add spices and stir one cup of water and cook for 20 minutes on medium heat. Simmer until juices are cooked off. Let meat cool and dry. Season to taste. Shred pork and fill each tortilla with pork saute, roll and secure with a toothpick. In another skillet, heat oil and fry each pork roll-up until golden on both sides. Serve with a hot sauce of choice.

Serves 6

Soft Beef Tacos
Tacos de Carne Picada Suaves

1/2 pound ground beef
Corn tortillas
Cooking oil
2 garlic cloves
1/8 teaspoon cumin seeds
1/8 teaspoon black peppercorns
2 cups lettuce, chopped
1/2 cups tomato, diced
1 cup cheddar cheese, grated
Salt
Pepper

Crush garlic cloves, cumin seeds, and peppercorns. Heat skillet and add oil. Brown and cook ground beef, add crushed spices. Season to taste. In another skillet, heat oil for the tortillas. Pass each tortilla on both sides and fold in half, do not leave in oil to fry.* Fill each tortilla with beef, lettuce, tomatoes and cheese.

*Corn tortillas may fried hard for crispy tacos, but more oil is needed.

Serves 4-5

Soft Beef Tacos 2
Tacos al Pastor

1/2 fajitas or beef skirts*
1/2 lemon
1/2 beer of choice
Corn tortillas
Cooking oil
2 garlic cloves
1/8 teaspoon cumin seeds
1/8 teaspoon black peppercorns
2 tablespoons tomato sauce
2 cups lettuce, chopped
1/2 cups tomato, diced
1 cup white, fresh cheese or farmer's, crumbled
Salt
Pepper
1 cup green sauce, see recipe

In a large bowl place fajitas and rub lemon on meat and then squeeze lemon juice to cover. Pour beer on meat and marinate in the refrigerator for at least 1 hour. (Any beef skirt marinate may be substituted. See Beef Skirt Recipes.)

Crush or grind garlic, cumin seeds and peppercorns. Heat skillet and add oil. Brown fajitas lightly and then add crushed spices. Add 1/4 cup of water and tomato sauce and stir. *If grilling fajitas, then stop here and grill as desired.* Cook until tender and juices are cooked off. Season to taste. Set aside and let cool, enough to handle. Place meat on a cutting board and chop meat as fine as possible. Keep warm. In another skillet, heat oil for the tortillas. Pass each tortilla on both sides and fold in half, do not leave in oil to fry.** Fill each tortilla with chopped beef, lettuce, tomatoes and cheese. Pour green sauce and serve immediately.

**Corn tortillas may fried hard for crispy tacos, but more oil is needed.

Serves 4-5

Soft Chicken Tacos
Tacos Suaves

1 chicken fryer, boiled, de-boned and shredded
Corn tortillas
Cooking oil
2 garlic cloves
1/8 teaspoon cumin seeds
1/8 teaspoon black peppercorns
1/4 cup tomato sauce
1/4 cup bell peppers, julienned
1/4 cup onions, chopped
2 cups lettuce, chopped
1/2 cups tomato, diced
Salt
Pepper

Boil, de-bone and shred chicken. Reserve the water. Crush garlic cloves, cumin seeds, and peppercorns. Heat skillet and add oil. Saute chicken with crushed spices, tomato sauce, bell peppers and onions. Season to taste. Add some chicken stock, then cook for a few minutes or until most of the juices are cooked off. In another skillet, heat oil for the tortillas. Pass each tortilla on both sides and fold in half, do not leave in oil to fry. Fill each tortilla with chicken saute, lettuce and tomatoes.

*Corn tortillas may fried hard for crispy tacos, but more oil is needed.

Serves 4-5

Stuffed Peppers
Chiles Rellenos

6 Poblano peppers
1 cup American cheese, grated
4 eggs
Salt
1 cup flour
Cooking oil

Optional: Picadillo (See recipe)

First make a slit in each pepper. Then on stove top or on a hot griddle roast peppers using tongs until all sides are blackened or blistered evenly. Place them in a bag and close until peppers are cool enough to handle. Peppers may also be placed in a bowl of ice water. Once peppers are cool, peel off skin and discard. Remove stem by cutting around the stem and dislodging stem and seeds. Fill with cheese or picadillo and set aside.

Separate eggs. First beat egg whites with a pinch of salt to form stiff peaks. In a separate bowl, beat yolks until thick. Mix egg whites and yolks on low speed. On a plate add flour and roll peppers. Heat a skillet and add oil. Dip floured peppers in egg mixture and fry until golden brown on both sides. Repeat until all peppers have been cooked. Serve with rice and beans.

Serves 6

Stuffed Red Peppers
Chile Dulce Relleno

4 red bell peppers
1/3 cup scallions, minced
1 tablespoon olive oil
1 garlic clove
1/4 teaspoon cumin seeds
1/8 teaspoon black peppercorns
1 cup pinto beans cooked and drained
2 tomatoes, diced
1 jalapeno pepper, chopped
2 tablespoons coriander leaves, chopped
1 teaspoon dried oregano
1 bay leaf
2 cups whole kernel corn, drained

Crush or grind garlic, cumin, and peppercorns. Heat a skillet and add oil. Saute scallions and crushed spices. To this add tomatoes, peppers, coriander, oregano, and bay leaf. Bring to a boil and then simmer for 10 minutes. Add the corn and cover for 8 minutes. Remove bay leaf and add beans. Stir and simmer on low heat.

Remove 1/2 inch off the top of each pepper. Discard seeds. Steam whole peppers until tender. Stuff each pepper equally with the mixture.

Serves 4

Tortillas filled with Cheese-Shortcut Quesadillas

6 flour tortillas
6 ounces white cheese of choice

On medium to high heat, heat *comal,* or griddle. Cut cheese in thin strips. Place strips of cheese in each tortilla and fold in half. Place tortilla filled with cheese on hot griddle. Toast each side until golden brown or until cheese oozes out.

Serves 3

NOTE: The *comal* is simply a Mexican griddle, which was probably first used to cook over an open flame or a wood burning stove. A modern version is made of cast iron and is designed to fit over a single or double eye of an electric or gas stove. This is one of the primary utensils used in making homemade tortillas.

Wheat Flour Tortillas
Tortillas de Trigo

2 cups wheat flour
1/3 cup shortening
1/4 teaspoon salt
1 1/2 tablespoons baking powder
1/2 cup hot water

In a large bowl add flour, salt and baking powder. Mix well with hands or whisk. Add shortening and knead thoroughly. Add warm water a little at a time until the dough starts to form. Knead well. Cover dough with plastic wrap or cloth. Allow to sit for 30 minutes. Separate dough into little balls, or *testales*, and knead each one. Before rolling dough, make sure to flour the rolling pin and board. Roll out each ball as thin as possible. Turn griddle(s) on medium to high heat. Cook each tortilla on both sides until brown spots have formed. Stack and cover. Compliment with any meal or eat as a snack.

Yields:10-12 tortillas

Index

To Order Additional Copies of

A Taste of Mexico
with Jozi Maldonado

Phone: 1-800-465-5225
Use Your Visa or Master Card

P.O. Box 531269
Harlingen, TX.
78553

The Castaway Company